WITHDRAWN

The European Family

THE MAKING OF EUROPE

Series Editor: Jacques Le Goff

The *Making of Europe* series is the result of a unique collaboration between five European publishers – Beck in Germany, Blackwell in Great Britain and the United States, Critica in Spain, Laterza in Italy and le Seuil in France. Each book will be published in all five languages. The scope of the series is broad, encompassing the history of ideas as well as of societies, nations and states to produce informative, readable, and provocative treatments of central themes in the history of the European peoples and their cultures.

Also available in this series

The European City
Leonardo Benevolo

The Rise of Western Christendom:
Triumph and Diversity 200–1000 AD
Peter Brown

The European Renaissance
Peter Burke

The Search for the Perfect Language
Umberto Eco

The Distorted Past: A
Reinterpretation of Europe
Josep Fontana

The European Family
Jack Goody

The Origins of European
Individualism
Aaron Gurevich

The Enlightenment
Ulrich Im Hof

The Population of Europe
Massimo Livi Bacci

Europe and the Sea
Michel Mollat du Jourdin

The Culture of Food
Massimo Montanari

Religion and Society in Modern
Europe
René Rémond

The Peasantry of Europe
Werner Rösener

States, Nations and Nationalism
Hagen Schulze

European Revolutions 1492–1992
Charles Tilly

In preparation

Democracy in European History
Maurice Agulhon

Migration and Culture
Klaus Bade

Women in European History
Gisela Bock

Europe and Islam
Franco Cardini

The Industrialization of Europe
Jurgen Kocka

The Law in European History
Peter Landau

The University in European History
Jacques Le Goff

The First European Revolution,
900–1200
R. I. Moore

The Frontier in European History
Krzysztof Pomian

The Birth of Modern Science
Paolo Rossi

The European Family
An Historico-Anthropological Essay

Jack Goody

BLACKWELL
Publishers

First published in 2000 by Blackwell Publishers and four other publishers: © 2000 Beck,
Munich (German); © 2000 Critica, Barcelona (Spanish); © 2000 Editions du Seuil, Paris
(French); © 2000 Laterza, Rome and Bari (Italian).

2 4 6 8 10 9 7 5 3 1

Blackwell Publishers Ltd
108 Cowley Road
Oxford OX4 1JF
UK

Blackwell Publishers Inc.
350 Main Street
Malden, Massachusetts 02148
USA

British Library Cataloguing in Publication Data

A CIP catalogue record for this book is available from the British Library.

Library of Congress Cataloging-in-Publication Data

Goody, Jack.
The European family : an historico-anthropological essay / Jack Goody.
p.   cm.—(Making of Europe)
Includes bibliographical references and index.
ISBN 0–631–20156–4 (hardbound : alk. paper)
1. Family—Europe—History. I. Title. II. Series.
HQ611.G665   2000
306.85'094—dc21   99-34410
                                                          CIP

Typeset in 11 on 12.5pt Sabon
by Grahame & Grahame Editorial, Brighton
Printed in Great Britain by
MPG Books Ltd, Bodmin, Cornwall

This book is printed on acid-free paper

Contents

Series Editor's Preface

Europe is in the making. This is both a great challenge and one that can be met only by taking the past into account – a Europe without history would be orphaned and unhappy. Yesterday conditions today; today's actions will be felt tomorrow. The memory of the past should not paralyze the present: when based on understanding it can help us to forge new friendships, and guide us towards progress.

Europe is bordered by the Atlantic, Asia, and Africa, its history and geography inextricably entwined, and its past comprehensible only within the context of the world at large. The territory retains the name given it by the ancient Greeks, and the roots of its heritage may be traced far into prehistory. It is on this foundation – rich and creative, united yet diverse – that Europe's future will be built.

The Making of Europe is the joint initiative of five publishers of different languages and nationalities: Beck in Munich; Blackwell in Oxford; Critica in Barcelona; Laterza in Rome; and le Seuil in Paris. Its aim is to describe the evolution of Europe, presenting the triumphs but not concealing the difficulties. In their efforts to achieve accord and unity the nations of Europe have faced discord, division, and conflict. It is no purpose of this series to conceal these problems: those committed to the European enterprise will not succeed if their view of the future is unencumbered by an understanding of the past.

The title of the series is thus an active one: the time is yet to come when a synthetic history of Europe will be possible. The books we shall publish will be the work of leading historians, by no means all European. They will address crucial aspects of European history in every field – political, economic, social, religious, and cultural. They will draw on that long historiographical tradition which stretches back to Herodotus, as well as on those conceptions and ideas which have transformed historical enquiry in the recent decades of the twentieth century. They will write readably for a wide public.

Our aim is to consider the key questions confronting those involved in Europe's making, and at the same time to satisfy the curiosity of the world at large: in short, who are the Europeans? where have they come from? whither are they bound?

Jacques Le Goff

Preface

The attempt to write an essay on 'the family in Europe' is clearly a gargantuan task. The questions go back to earliest times when the sources start meagerly. They become increasingly more complex (and hence less accessible), while the internal differences are many. However, the roots and development of the very basic set of features concerned with the family, kinship and marriage is of interest to us all since it forms the setting in which we spend so much of our lives. Some general treatment is certainly called for.

My own qualifications are hardly the usual ones. I am not a historian, nor a specialist in European studies, but rather a comparativist – an anthropologist by training who has carried out intensive fieldwork in Africa and less intensive enquiries in Asia. I am not setting out to offer a continuous narrative account; that would be impossible in the space I have been allotted. Mine is rather an analytical approach. I was encouraged to take up controversial issues in the treatment of the family in Europe, which means referring to the work of specific authors, often commenting upon my own earlier work. In order to preserve the historical dimension, and to consider problems of change and continuity, I have tried to spotlight significant periods and to discuss the controversial issues that surround them. This I can do only from my standpoint; the reader should be aware that opinions differ quite radically.

But it has also been necessary to pursue some themes outside these chronological limitations, in order to examine a topic such as dowry or sectarian differences. That procedure may also involve jumping from place to place and from time to time in a way likely to unsettle professional historians.

It is clear that in a short essay I cannot deal with all the variations over the history of a large continent. Indeed the task would be quite beyond me. That means taking individual cases as paradigms, even though one case can never be an exact replica of another. As I am reminded by a learned commentator, E. P. Thompson referred to both anthropology and history as subjects of context. True. But it is also inevitable that one goes beyond context in the concepts one uses (e.g., 'family') and in the ideas one elaborates, especially if it is thought essential to emphasize a comparative discussion in order to counter the multiplicity of ethnocentric assumptions that surrounds a particular topic.

Finally, there is obviously much more I could have written, developed, had I not been constrained by editorial demands concerning length and audience. This is a general anthropological-historical essay and has to be read as such, not as a historical narrative.

My standpoint means concentrating upon the literature and the languages I know. If England remains a central focus, it does so not because I follow the line of many historians in thinking that there the family and surrounding attitudes and sentiments differed fundamentally from the rest of the continent in ways that promoted 'modernization', 'capitalism' or 'industrialization'. My aim is quite the contrary, to use the ample material on that country to bring out the general aspects of the analysis of domestic institutions in the West (and sometimes in the East as well, or even of families more widely distributed). I have therefore tried to emphasize a comparative analytical perspective in the historical context.

Most historical accounts, quite apart from neglecting wider comparison, fail to include the sociological present. That seems to me intrinsic not only to the narrative but to the analysis; we need to understand for example what has happened to the so-called 'affective family' in order to assess whether it was really so affectionate. This I have tried to do based on work on the contemporary situation in Europe I am pursuing with Juliet Mitchell.

I came back to European studies because I was convinced that scholars had taken too narrow a view of their task in attempting to deal with the history of the European family. Such an undertaking requires a theoretical and comparative dimension because optimally we need to examine any particular system as one in the range of possible forms and to be aware of what other work has been done on the distribution, for example, of family types, of developmental cycles. Only then can we assess the claims made by historians. Of course all societies, indeed all families, are unique. But here historians are discussing broad aspects like childhood or maternal love which some see not only as particular to Europe but as significantly related to the processes of modernization in a global sense.

Editorial considerations have made me eliminate many of the references to 'other cultures', as well as those on Europe not directly concerned with my text. Fuller bibliographies will be found in some of the general works I mention below. To others, whose names I have omitted, I offer my apologies but the literature is too vast to survey adequately in such a short volume.

In treating these issues I am necessarily heavily indebted to the work of other scholars who have served to focus my interest or provided me with material. For the earlier period I attempt to update my earlier study of *The Development of Marriage and the Family in Europe* (1983) which has been commented on by a number of Roman historians of the family.[1] For the other periods, too, I have depended upon a selection of works that have seemed important to me.[2] My thanks are especially due to Olwen Hufton, Juliet Mitchell, Ulinka Rublack, David Sabean, Martine Segalen, Keith Wrightson and anonymous readers for their extensive comments on the manuscript, as well as the editorial advice of Jacques Le Goff, the help of many friends in suggesting reading and the assistance of those who have been involved in preparing the manuscript.

Jack Goody
Cambridge, January 1999

1
The Beginnings

The past of the European family influences its present, both its continuities and its discontinuities. There is much talk today of the end of the family or for an earlier period of invention of childhood or the emergence of the 'affective family' (each implying radical change from what went before). The thrust of this account is that there is no end to the family; some kind of sexual coupling and child care is essential for the vast majority of humankind. Non-reproductive families are certainly more common than in the past, but they constitute a minority in Europe as elsewhere. Meanwhile new reproductive techniques seem hardly likely to replace for most of humankind the pleasures of sex.

Changes in its structure have taken place over time but I would challenge whether these are best described in terms such as the emergence of the nuclear or affective family, of parental or conjugal love. There have been important continuities as well as discontinuities, if only because the demands of social reproduction have hitherto promoted some kind of small family structure as well as a strong link within and between the generations. Too much has been made of the distinctiveness of the modern family, especially in the West, some features of which have been in place since the late Roman times as well as in other parts of the world.[1]

The early roots of the European family lie in the classical Mediterranean civilizations of Greece and Rome as well as in the

Germanic and Celtic tribal societies that dominated much of the north and west of the continent when those civilizations flourished to the south. Both strands have been held responsible for significant aspects of the family in later Europe, especially Rome for family law and the Teutonic tribes for features such as the bilateral reckoning of kin and the stress on 'individualism'. Classical legal texts are not always easy to interpret from a behavioural standpoint, while for the early Germans we are largely dependent upon the writings of outsiders, since they themselves were non-literate. Although some of the specific attributions need to be corrected, Romanists and Germanists, classicists and tribalists, are surely both right in perceiving influences on later family structures. But some of these features, such as the endowment of women at marriage, were not confined to European societies. Moreover, the greatest influence of all resulted from the advent of Christianity, ultimately from the Near East, when the church, in the process of converting, introduced a number of changes that transformed the earlier patterns of domestic life.

Common Features of Family Life

Before elaborating these topics, let us begin by considering certain general points about family, kinship and marriage, derived from comparative studies, that we need to recall in dealing with Europe. Firstly we know of virtually no society in the history of humanity where the elementary or nuclear family was not important, in the vast majority of cases as a co-residential group.

Secondly, even where that family is not jurally monogamous, it often is in practice; and the basic unit of production and reproduction is always relatively small. The variations in size of households cover quite a narrow band.

Thirdly, and consequently, even where unilineal descent groups such as the patrilineal *gens* exist, as in Rome, there is always a reckoning of consanguinal (bilateral) ties through both parents, including the one through whom descent is not reckoned (what Fortes called 'complementary filiation'). For example even in patrilineal societies, the mother's brother is always an important figure and that is no indication of an earlier matrilineal organization.

Fourthly, in no society are the ties between mother and child (and in the vast majority, between father and child) unimportant, sentimentally and jurally, even though in some ideological contexts those ties may be played down (for example, among the upper class in the literature in earlier Mediterranean societies).

From these features we can conclude on general grounds that there is no serious sense in which Europe, let alone capitalism, has invented the elementary or nuclear family or even the small household. Different societies give different weight to domestic relationships and the wider ranges of kinship reckoning also vary. In classical times, Greece and Rome both gave some emphasis to unilineal descent groups (patrilineal clans and lineages) but these largely disappeared in Europe under the impact of the German invaders with their bilateral kindreds and under pressure from the Christian church which weakened all wider kinship groups by effectively limiting their extent and initiating an alternative system of ritual relations, of godparenthood. This weakening suited both the ecclesia and the feudal lords. Gradually such wider bilateral ties shrank in importance until, today, with a few exceptions, the effective range of kin relations in Europe is rarely more than the descendants of a grandparental couple, that is, immmediate uncles and aunts (parent's siblings) and their children (first cousins).

Did this change already take place in Roman society from the second century BCE?[2] We may be suffering here from lack of adequate information since it is not easy to visualize a society with agnatic (unilineal) descent groups that does not also have a bilateral reckoning of kin. Since we know that the Romans had the *gens*, the important question in this case is not whether they also recognized bilateral ties but why did unilineal groupings disappear? The diminution of the importance of the *gens* and the *familia* has been alleged to have favoured 'the emergence of two other groups, the complex family, created by remarriage, and the cognate family or cognates, centered on one person, and including relatives in both the male and female lines'.[3] But no reason is offered for the diminution nor for the timing of the final disappearance of the *gens*. That fact does not seem to have been considered as a problem. In Europe descent groups (clans) that were more than patronymics (that is, surnames) are found in Ireland as was the case in the Highlands of Scotland, and in some mountainous areas of the Balkans (for example, Albania). Interestingly there was some recognition of what I have called *lignages* in Italy, for example among the nobility in Florence[4] and in Genoa, as well as in some other Mediterranean areas such as Corfu.[5] I use this word to distinguish them from African *lineages*, which kept male property within the group, whereas with diverging devolution it was always being dispersed through women by marriage, involving a different relationship between group and property. Did these collectivities have any continuity with earlier descent groups? In other parts of Europe, clans and lineages had either disappeared or had never existed. There seems no evidence that the Anglo-Saxons ever had anything other than bilateral kindreds (of a variety of kinds) which regulated defence and offence in a similar way to unilineal clans elsewhere. Did other Germanic peoples have unilineal groups? The early legal codes make that possibility seem unlikely.

Nor did Europe, as has been widely claimed, invent childhood, nor yet affection (even 'love') between husband and wife nor parents and children. Parents have always mourned their children and spouses each other. Mourning behaviour, like affection, is universal and it is only the crudest history of mentalities, combined with an overpowering and ignorant ethnocentricism that suggests otherwise. Once again there are differences of emphasis, but emotions are poor material for historians who are likely to make untold mistakes in assessing them.[6] The care of children within a conjugal relationship which is defined by relatively exclusive sexual and marital rights is a quasi-universal. Mourning for children is one consequence; so too is emotional attachment between spouses. It is wrong (in my opinion) to see these features as coming into being in the sixteenth, seventeenth, or nineteenth centuries. This cannot be correct,[7] just as it is also wrong to seek their origin in later Rome. There is undoubtedly a 'history' of emotions but not in the crude, unilineal terms proposed by many European historians.

Eurasia and the Bronze Age

Some of the features of family life that have been seen as unique to Europe are simply variants of universal human features, like mother love and sexual attraction. Others are characteristic not of Europe but of Eurasia as a whole, of the great civilizations that emerged during the Bronze Age.

The Bronze Age created new conditions that affected the family right across Eurasia; such an assumption runs directly contrary to the Marxist, Weberian and predominant European view that Orient and Occident diverged at an earlier unspecified period – a notion that fits easily into the ideas not only of the western public but of the vast majority of European historians and social scientists, that there was some longstanding differences between the two that were relevant to the later process of modernization.

What was it about the Bronze Age? I have suggested that it introduced new forms of stratification, in contrast for example with Africa, that were based on the ownership of land. The land was now capable of being cultivated by more intensive methods (by ploughing, irrigation, etc.) producing a larger surplus above subsistence that could sustain the crafts and specialisms of urban living.

These changes of a socio-economic kind had profound effects on family structures. Clearly other socio-economic changes also affected family structures, the slave economies of the classical world, the feudalism of the Middle Ages. The main discussion among modern scholars has obviously centred upon what happened since the Renaissance and the effects associated with the development of mercantile capitalism, with the Reformation and above all with the coming of industrial capitalism towards the end of the eighteenth century. Those shifts have inevitably influenced the formation and operation of domestic groups which earlier constituted units of production and now no longer did for much of the population, although property remained important for the majority; as units of reproduction, however, they have been less clearly affected until the present century since in that sphere they had a measure of autonomy which provided them with a degree of continuity. As units of reproduction, families had a permanent job to do both at an individual and at a societal level. Then again there was the very important factor of religious ideology and practice, as we see in contemporary debates about abortion, which partially insulated these areas from the pressures of the major socio-economic changes. It is an intertwining of these considerations that sets the scene for any treatment of the history of the European family.

The major societies of Europe and Asia practised an advanced agriculture using the plough and irrigation, so the differences on this score were not as marked. There is good reason to set aside some of the more extreme views of the differences in kinship systems between east and west, embodied in the arguments of those who see the pre-existing European family as linked to the modern achievements of that continent, as being very distinct from the wider-ranging and often unilineal systems of the East.[8] But while each society or sub-group displayed its own selection of kinship variables, they also had much in common. And even the choices themselves can sometimes be seen as offering different solutions to similar problems, for example, in relation to strategies of heirship or to household management.[9]

A large part of the continent certainly acquired some unity by the widespread adoption of Christian norms by peoples with very different backgrounds. This relative uniformity touched upon many aspects of family life, such as the marriage prohibition on kin, on affines and on that newly invented category of 'ritual kin', god-relatives, spiritual kin. But the later religious divide between Catholic and Protestant also becomes important with regard to the family, especially for prohibited degrees of marriage (at least in England and among Huguenots in France), and for their complement, the 'incest taboo', as well as for divorce which becomes possible, but not common, in all Protestant countries except England.

A consideration of the particular features of Christian Europe has nothing to do with the usual notions of the Uniqueness of the West in relation to modernization, which involve seeing others (especially Asia) as backward, unable to make the necessary breakthrough.[10] Uniqueness can obviously only be established by systematic comparative enquiry, not by ethnocentric speculation.

Given these general features of post-Bronze-Age Eurasia, we need to ask why we should isolate Europe for the study of family institutions. For it is only a fictional continent, not bounded in any decisive geographical way but only by an imaginary frontier along the Bosphorus and the Urals.[11] The basic reason has to do with Europe conceived firstly as the Christian continent and secondly as leading the world in modernization, industrialization and capitalism. Both notions suggest a search for unique factors, including the family, in the former case as a consequence, in the latter possibly as cause of its lead. Regarding the first factor it has to be remembered that the continent had its non-Christian roots, both Germanic (plus Celts and other 'tribes') and classical (both Greece and Rome), and that Christianity itself owed much to the traditions of the Jewish Old Testament. Moreover, the continent continued to include substantial minorities, of Jews and Muslims, not to speak of Gypsies and other travellers, who were committed to alternative beliefs and ways of living, and of more recent migrants from the West Indies, from North Africa, from Africa south of the Sahara and from India. Regarding the second, Europe, even Christian Europe, formed part of the wider Eurasian area which had a considerable number of important features in common, developed or inherited from post-Bronze-Age cultures, such as the endowment of women and the associated 'women's property complex'.[12] In most societies women have been considered 'jural minors', anyhow until recently, and that has been an aspect of their frequent subordination and even oppression. Their position has varied not only from society to society and from time to time, but also by class and depending upon the composition of their natal families. In post-Bronze-Age societies a woman without brothers might be an heiress, capable of attracting a man to live with her and 'of wearing the trousers' as many a peasant proverb points out. An heiress was superior in important ways to a penniless man, even to many a younger son in her own class. While this system of endowment was modified by the Christian church to its own design, the considerations regarding family strategies (as distinct from charity) that gave rise to that complex of variables remained potentially active. This complex of variables emerged as countervailing forces at various points in European history, modifying in turn the prescriptions of the Church, as in the history of Henry VIII of England.

Mode of livelihood, whether of landless, peasant, merchant or noble, greatly influenced family life, for example as when many rural workers shifted from agricultural production to cottage industry. In the latter case they were no longer subject to the same constraints that peasant agricultural production entailed, constraints of limited resources to feed and distribute to children, the need to adjust land to labour, the constraints (and advantages) of inheriting rights to property, which profoundly affected relations between the generations. 'Inherited property as the "tangible" determinant of household formation and family structure receded in the face of the overwhelming importance of the family as a unit of labour'.[14] Women's earnings encouraged early marriage and the employment available for children promoted larger families.[14] It meant that the women were often the 'vanguard of peasant household industries'[15] but more often there was a merging of the division of labour without, apparently, all the disastrous consequences that some foresaw in its disappearance.

Internal Differences

While the influences of Christianity and the Bronze Age were strong, there were many variations in family structure over time and over place. No one is suggesting uniformity. A recent book on the Italian family since Antiquity takes up the question of the diversity of the European family and the problem of generalization.[16] Rightly so. But it fails to replace what the authors see as unsatisfactory paradigms, developmental and comparative, by anything else. My intention is to try and provide some very general suggestions that go beyond the mere assertion of diversity, which seems unconstructive. For what appears infinitely variable and flexible from within does not always seem so from without. That is partly why one needs a wider perspective. In that context, for example, the absence of divorce and the presence of god-parenthood stand out as important features of Christian Europe which distinguish these societies from many of the surrounding and many of the earlier ones. Some of these factors are not in themselves entirely unique to Europe – divorce is equally impossible in India, ritual kinship of different kinds exists elsewhere. But in Europe these features are part of a package introduced by the Christian church.

Inheritance systems vary widely in Europe. But there are some widespread factors that distinguish much of that continent not so much from the rest of Asia but from Africa, mainly in the devolution of parental property to daughters as well as to sons (as inheritance, as dowry or as both). And linked to this there is the devolution to brotherless daughters as heiresses before collateral males (cousins); the latter are by and large excluded. Both these factors distinguish European from African inheritance in a radical way. That I have argued is a feature of post-Bronze-Age societies and related to their economy and system of stratification in which it was deemed essential to preserve the status of daughters as well as of sons (in other words, the status of the whole natal family), as is not at all the case in Africa. The very fact of partitioning property between sons and daughters may tend to produce smaller families (that is, numbers of offspring) than when a couple are aiming for a maximum holding of males.

Some of these difference may arise from the shift between functionally similar institutions which does not necessarily require the intervention of any major extraneous event. In examining strategies of heirship, the act of adoption can have as an alternative, at least in those cases where there are daughters, the possibility of transmitting property to a daughter's son, in apparent breach of the dominant agnatic inheritance. Or, what is effectively the same, the contraction of a filiacentric (uxorilocal) union, where the incoming son-in-law acts as a temporary manager for the daughter and her parental property; as the French say, 'il fait le gendre'.

When this practice occurred at the end of Antiquity, it has been seen as indicating a shift away from agnatic reckoning to consanguinity ('blood') and alliance (or marriage).[17] In some ways adoption placed a greater emphasis on direct descent. However daughters too are agnates so that blood (even agnatic blood) was being favoured rather than the 'fictional' kin created by adoption. I doubt if we should account for such a change from adoption in these general terms but rather look for more specific reasons. One of these would be the growing influence of the Christian church at this period, for Salvianus was already fulminating against adoption in the fifth century on the grounds that such an act deprived God of his own things and the church of property. In any case this particular substitution of the heiress could obviously take place only in those cases where daughters had been born to the family.

Not all of Europe was equally influenced by Christianity. Early in the eighth century most of the Iberian penisula was conquered by Moorish armies and became part of the World of Islam. So too did Malta, Sicily and sections of the Balkans, which remain Muslim to this day. The influx of Jews and Gypsies also gave rise to communities whose family system differed in significant ways from the rest of Europe.[18]

Regarding the Islamic presence there has been a tendency to stress the continuities of life in Andalusia with that of the earlier pre-Islamic inhabitants. But another current insisted upon the substantial differences.[19] The Muslims brought along the notion of 'tribe' and although these larger units tended to become less important from the tenth century onwards, the relevance of patrilineal lineages remained. Within such lineages preference was given to close kinship marriages, especially of a man to the father's brother's daughter, as is customary throughout Islam.

One of the arguments for the supposed continuity (and hence the rejection of Islamic influence) has been the claim that Andalusian women had greater freedom than others in the Arab world and that this freedom was part of the heritage from those earlier populations. But as elsewhere religious leaders decreed that women should be secluded and wear the veil; the freedom characterized the behaviour not so much of ordinary folk but rather of the *quiyan* or cultured slaves who sang, danced and engaged in conversation at male gatherings, and whose role resembled that of the *geisha* of Japan and the *hetaira* of Ancient Greece.

Christianity

Are there any general features that are specific to the European family? That depends upon when and to some extent where one starts. In order to make any such statement we have to take a comparative perspective, looking at the contrast or similarities with Africa and Asia. Continental distribution is not in itself the major factor in any differences. Africa south of the Sahara differs significantly from both Europe and Asia because it had a simpler productive system which had implications for the nature of ownership and of stratification; and that in turn affects the nature of inheritance, marriage and ties of kinship.

Europe began to differ substantially from Asia and from the surrounding Mediterranean when it adopted Christianity with its very specific selection of new norms. And those new rules were not simply diacritical features used to differentiate themselves, for example, from Jews and pagans (though this they often did) but were introduced for specific reasons connected with the establishment and maintenance of the church as a major organization in society.

If we look at the long run of the history of the family in Europe, a number of features stand out. The influence of the Catholic church on marriage and the family, especially in the context of its accumulation of funds which were shifted there from family and municipality, had important consequences.[20] The effects of these specific norms and general pressures ran against the strategies of heirship that Eurasian families had used to continue their lines and to prolong the association between kin and property which preserved their hierachical status. There were recurrent conflicts throughout European history between ecclesiastical and lay interests in the accumulation of funds, just as there were between the interests of church and state in matters well beyond the family but arising out of the church's emergence as a 'great organization'.

Resistance

Since some of these strategies were set aside, one would expect an undercurrent of resistance to the demands of the church and this is exactly what one finds. One would also expect other religions with different priorities to be more accommodating to these underlying concerns, closer to the 'Eurasian tradition' and that was true of the Jewish and to some extent of the Muslim groups in Europe, who for example permitted, even encouraged, close marriages as well as allowing divorce. Such accommodations also became characteristic of 'heretical' movements which broke away from the dominant Catholic and orthodox churches. Eventually the most influential of these movements, Protestantism, dispensed with some of these restrictions. Consequently one of the major differences in family structure lay between religious communities, for example, in the specific role provided for widows in Catholic communities, on which Florence Nightingale remarked. An even greater change was to occur when the religious-backed norms were affected by an ongoing secularization and the decreasing role of ecclesiastical courts, in England from the eighteenth century, which eventually allowed greater freedom, among other things, in changing marital partners.

The nature of the imposition by the church of important norms concerning marriage and the family which were then internalized or otherwise accepted in various degrees by the inhabitants of Christian Europe, can be seen in the way such rules were evaded in the course of European history. There is always deviance from behavioural injunctions but that to which I refer forms a regular pattern pointing to links with the practice of Asia and even of pre-Christian Europe, in so far as we can reconstruct them. When religion becomes of less significance because of secularization or conversion to some other cult, as it did after the Renaissance and Reformation, those norms will obviously change. That change has occurred in the case, for example, of the approval of artificial birth control, of abortion and of divorce. Birth control was certainly practised in France as in Catholic Italy but practice was private whereas divorce was public. Since the regulation of divorce shifted in many cases from ecclesiastical to state courts, it has become increasingly available, opening up the possibility of remarriage, except for the members of a few congregations. Even today the inheritance of the English crown has up to now depended upon the avoidance of divorce and remarriage.

It is difficult to argue that this shift is related to any of the factors that are often seen as encouraging the promotion of a close nuclear family deemed to be essential to capitalism[21] or to the modern affective family[22], for it surely points in quite another direction, that is, to the break-up of marriages, to the disappearance of religious sanctions. The direction of change is more ambiguous than many such theories imply. Prohibitions are being lifted without being replaced by any alternative norms, except that of providing more freedom of choice for the adult partners. The result produces many of the complexities of contemporary family life.

The secularization that promoted this change was part of a wider shift in society that accompanied the development of knowledge and educational systems after the Renaissance in the context of the flourishing of merchant cultures. Knowledge assisted the invention of new technologies, as did the increasing wealth that accompanied the exploration and conquest of overseas territories, the opening up of European trade on a world-wide basis, a process that has been curiously described as the 'primitive' accumulation of capital.

I argue that the secularization of which I speak is not at all the equivalent of modernization, though many sociologists have seen it in this way. Modernity is a slippery concept, with no firm base in time or place and with no clearly defined characteristics; with its counterpart 'traditional' its features differ with each authority. Secularization on the other hand refers to the decay of the influence of the church, the shift of family affairs to lay courts, the dissolution of the monasteries as well as the increased emphasis on secular ideologies and explanations. That process was one aspect of the Englightenment and growth of knowledge in eighteenth century Europe but had long been a prominent element of Confucianism in the Far East and the established Lokāyata trend in India. Of course, scepticism and agnosticism were features of both western and eastern thought over the centuries but in the West they became a dominant concern only in the eighteenth-century, although the Catholic pressures on family life were obviously modified by the widespread movement towards Reform in the sixteenth.

The concern with secularization is not only a matter of ideology but of property. When the Catholic church ceased to hold or acquire property as it had done earlier, its relationship with the rest of society, and especially with the family, necessarily changed. The less the church acquired, the more remained in private or in public hands.

Continuities and Discontinuities

This discussion returns us to the question of continuity and change in family structures. There are two approaches to the history of the family in Europe.[23] One emphasizes the continuities in the family, particularly in England, as critical to the process of modernization, whereas the other tends to view the causal link as taking the opposite course. In reality there was both continuity and change, and the main job is to try and draw a balance between the two.

What are the kind of pressures that result in a particular set of family relationships? There is always 'tradition', persistence, inertia. A particular system may be well adapted to other features of the society in a vaguely functional way. As we have seen, the job of reproduction has some basic parameters (sex, care of children, etc.). Once a set of practices has become established, it tends to be transmitted from generation to generation. Domestic groups are ones that organize living space and also serve as units of reproduction and consumption; as such they have some functions that are relatively autonomous, not entirely subordinated to wider changes, and that have to be fulfilled in all or most human societies, even though the working out of those functions may take different forms. But there are clearly some important changes that are broadly related to productive systems since domestic groups in agricultural societies are often units of production. These relationships also respond to the imperatives of church, of state (and its judicial system) and to some extent of landlords, as well as of the market.

Equally it seems to me mistaken to look at these features as purely English or even European phenomena; both the discontinuity and the continuity arguments are misplaced in that context. The arguments relate to the earlier discussion of Malinowski, Westermarck and others about the universality of the elementary or nuclear family.[24] While there may indeed be some situations/structures such as that of the Nayar of southwestern India which one agrees to see as lying outside these definitional boundaries, there is no doubt that the vast majority of human societies are built upon social-economic and affectionate relationships within the couple/child unit. This relationship emerges very clearly in funeral arrangements; the 'indifference' thesis, the notion that earlier societies, other cultures and other classes neglected their children, which has been adopted by some historians of 'mentalities', is disastrously ethnocentric and thoroughly misleading.

The main variables with which I deal, namely, economic and religious, operate on a pan-European scale. What is remarkable in recent changes in the family in Europe is the way these have taken place, not necessarily at the same time or same speed, throughout the continent. Other writers, concentrating on 'mentalities' or upon demographic factors, have often dwelt on differences between the regions of Europe, especially those writers who try to relate such variables to the advent of 'modernization' in one country (primarily England) or in one area (western Europe). The attempt to define mentalities on such a basis is, as will be discussed, less than adequate, while some of the demographic differences such as household size are less clear cut, and possibly less relevant, than have been maintained. On the other hand a late age of marriage for both sexes and the associated practice of unmarried in-living servants is certainly a general feature of European regimes dating from the late Middle Ages that has to be borne in mind.

I pursue a number of arguments in the chapters that follow but I have been principally interested in following up the idea that many of the early rules introduced by Christians, in opposition to the dominant Eurasian mode, helped the church to accumulate property at the expense of families and of wider kinship groups. If the church's influence was so great, the process of secularization that was encouraged by the New Learning of the Renaissance led to the modification of these particular rules, initially in some Protestant countries. Subsequently, when agriculture was supplemented by proto-industrialization and then by industrialization, the family was no longer tied to access to land in the same way and in the end rarely a productive unit. Those transformations had radical effects on domestic life and were pushed further by the Second Industrial Revolution later in the nineteenth century and by the socio-economic changes (or Third Industrial Revolution) that followed the Second World War. Those are the main factors that I examine in the chapters that follow.

2

The Heritage of Greece and Rome

We can discover little about the family in the pre-classical period in Europe. By definition we can only reconstruct in any concrete way the kinship systems of peoples with writing. That restricts us to the Greeks and Romans, peripherally the Cretans and, for comparison, other eastern Mediterraneans. As far as the classical family is concerned, the bulk of texts are literary for Greece and legal for Rome. It is on the latter that we will concentrate.[1] For the rest of Europe we are dependent upon what those sources tell us about Germanic and other peoples, together with the fragmentary references that we can reconstruct after the advent of writing with the coming of the Romans and especially of Christianity with its attacks on local practices.

Greece and the Dowry

Although Ancient Greece contributed so much to European culture and Roman law became so central in its public disputes, at the level of the family classical civilization did not leave a very notable heritage. Continuities and parallels there were but most of these were not specifically tied to classical societies. The dowry, for example, existed in Greece, where women were endowed and became heiresses in the absence of brothers (*epiklerates*), thus breaking with the hegemonic possession of property by male members of the lineage, a breach that radically differentiates major Eurasian societies from African descent groups.

So it was also important not only in the classical Mediterranean but in the other major Eurasian societies. In these cultures women received a portion of the conjugal fund of their parents, which is clearly one reason why certain of their marriages were entered into with close kin; for example, the heiress in Greece had to make what is also the preferred Islamic union with the father's brother's son in order to keep the property within the clan. But there was another relevant aspect. The Roman dowry system was partly designed to insure the woman against the severe economic consequences of divorce.[2] That was precisely the situation in Islam and Judaism down to recent times and is of course associated with those cultures in which marriage is not considered as inevitably permanent. The dowry certainly performed that function in countries where divorce was permitted, but it existed too in those such as Hindu India where marriages rarely ended except by death. However, in the case of final dissolution the dowry (or the dower) still served to support widows and to make them partially independent of both their affinal and their natal kin.

The dowry continued to dominate marriages in Europe even when divorce became virtually unknown. It was part of a wider set of family features shared with other societies in Eurasia, which included, I suggest, the presence of a small nuclear core, the conjugal pair endowed independently at marriage. This nucleus formed the base of the kinship system and was structured, in important ways, along the lines of later families in Europe. Changes of course occurred but the fact that Freud turned to Oedipus as a model for the analysis of intra-familial relationships indicates that we understand what is happening in Greek tragedies and in Homer in ways that would be inconceivable were there not a common core.

The existence of a dowry and the parallel endowment of men, but not always at marriage, meant that the marital pair was separated in significant ways from their respective natal groups by being set up with a conjugal fund that was in some limited sense under their control. Its presence tended to favour the establishment of distinct units, usually within a wider social and residential frame, as well as a measure of delay in taking such a step. That is not to say that all dowry societies have small households and late marriage, but there are underlying forces that push in these directions.

Unilineal Clans and Bilateral Families

Early Greek and Roman society is often seen as strongly clan-based, employing unilineal methods of reckoning kinship. In the Greek case this reckoning has been thought by some to have earlier been matrilineal, traced through women alone,[3] and in the Roman case agnatic, through men alone. The evidence for these early periods is thin and the methodology often dubious.[4] It is frequently contaminated by ideas of both actors and observers about the general progression of human societies from say matrilineal to patrilineal to bilateral reckoning. I do not totally discount some progression of this kind, although whatever took place is much more complex than such simplistic schemes suggest. What is relevant in the present context is the span of time over which any such changes occurred, for the perspective tends to get drastically foreshortened in an unrealistic manner, with for example any stress on the maternal being taken as an index (or 'survival') of the matrilineal. For the time when we have reasonably adequate sources, the kinship system seems much more complex than such a progression would suggest. For Rome, it has been claimed that 'Contemporary evidence for the second century BC. indicates that the strictly agnatic principles of early law were giving way to bilateral kinship reckoning'.[5] Given the nature of the evidence, we are entitled to ask how accurately the early laws represented the kinship system. Virtually all societies with patrilineal clans (for example the *gens*) also acknowledge bilateral ties, traced through both parents, which are implicit in the duality of procreation and parenting. Where you have agnates, you also have cognates; the two are not alternatives. That duality is also found with matrilineal clans; with the possible exception of the earlier Nayar of Malabar, in all such societies the role of the father is important. What we may be seeing in Rome is not so much changing kinship but a more adequate recognition in the written record of what actually existed in practice.

The norm is said to have been for Roman children to be brought up in the household of the father, to whose family they belonged. Indeed a mother might have a duty to contribute to their support even when they were not living with her. However it was proper for babies to remain with the mother for a limited period.[6] But while early custody might be with the mother, later in life it was definitely in the father's hands.

The bilateral question is raised for a much later period in the suggestion that Roman aristocratic families of the late fifth and early sixth centuries constituted groups based on principles of consanguinity and alliance rather than on the agnation of the Roman *gens*, although the latter still had its place in the legal code.[7] 'The agnatic *gens* as a fundamental element in Roman social and political organisation had disappeared long before, during the Empire', even though the extreme conservatism of legal codes meant that the change from agnatic to cognatic principles was not fully recognised until the code of Justinian was formulated.[8] But as we see there is no exclusive opposition between these two sets of principles; indeed alliance and descent, unilineality and complementary filiation, must necessarily co-exist, though they may receive differential stress in different societies or at different times. While it may well be that the agnatic component of the Roman family was losing its strength, there is an absence of adequate analysis either of the process or of the reasons for this, other than it represented part of the vague progress towards modernization.

The view that there had been a period marked by the complete dominance of the agnatic *gens* is, as I have suggested, highly questionable. The early codes are very selective and cannot be held to give a full account of the kinship system; for that we need dispute cases. Those first writings are highly deceptive and by the time we get to the fuller statements of Justinian we have to take Christian influences into the reckoning. Of the legal changes introduced at that time it has been said that in 543 Justinian invalidated 'all distinctions between agnates and cognates' in matters of succession.[9] In fact the privileged status of *agnatio* and *cognatio* seems to have been slowly eroded over the previous centuries. At the same time the notion of *consanguinitas* changed from a paternally-oriented definition of siblings to one related to cognation (bilaterality), that is to consanguines in the more usual sense (which had long been the meaning in everyday speech). That notion is especially clear in the texts of canon law on the prohibited degrees of marriage, constituting 'a striking departure from . . . Roman civil law' where the term was only used in connection with inheritance and succession;[10] the figurative representation of these prohibitions was referred to as *arbor consanguinitatis*. Neither of these developments speaks directly to the disappearance of the *gens*, since the existence of descent groups (and even more of patronymics) of this kind is perfectly consistent with the recognition of ties through the mother. But it does of course represent a modification of the Roman kinship universe, at least at the level of the written legal codes.

Did the *gens* disappear entirely? In Italy at a later period, some significance was given to unilineal structures among the aristocracy. However these groups seem to be not so much a continuation as a reinvention. In any case the 'lineages' of fifteenth-century Florence were accompanied by a set of ego-orientated relationships which recall 'the open bilateral groups of the high Middle Ages, frequently described before the patrilineal lineage was consolidated.'[11] In other words there was no question of those lineages being 'survivals' of the Roman *gens*; they were products of the urban society of a much later period.

Increasing Individualism?

The argument about the nature of kin groups or groupings is associated with those about the nature of family. As I have suggested some of the supposed changes in later Roman society may be due to fuller records, which amplified the nature of practical forms of kinship, family and marriage. Such amplification may have given rise to notions about the increased emphasis on ties through both parents, or on smaller family households or on individualism or indeed on love. While there was certainly some movement, the idea that these features did not exist earlier was undoubtedly mistaken and part of the general view, often held by the actors as well as by the observers, that there had been a shift away from collective institutions to more individualistic ones. Indeed the same process in burial rituals, from collective to "individualizing", has been seen to occur at the start of the Bronze Age over most of Europe (suggesting the development of social stratification). There may well have been a change in burial practice over this period but this description is painfully inadequate; even hunter-gatherers individualize death and burial. Like much of this use of collective–individual terminology, the conceptualization is grossly misleading. Nevertheless the usage is constantly echoed in studies of European kinship, the terms being used to describe the changes that took place in later Rome, in the early modern period or with industrialization. Movement there was but the descriptive terms are often inadequate and the changes were ones of degree rather than of kind.

Marriage and the Family

In the same spirit some historians of the Roman family have seen an increasing value attached to marriage and to children with the passage of time. This change has been attributed by some to Christianity, by others to the pre-Christian empire,[12] while yet others see any judgement as being too difficult to make.[13] I tend to agree with the latter, that the criteria chosen are very culture-bound. In all societies parents (especially mothers) display some attachment to children and to the unions that produce them; it is a condition of their human existence and their continuity. Making such discriminations on a society-wide level is rarely easy or satisfactory.

Children

Other historians have commented on the difficulties of using primary and secondary sources on children, such as personal diaries and advice literature. It has been pointed out how intractable the analysis of any body of documents of this kind can be; so untidy is it, so variable, so contradictory in its dogmas and doctrines, so capricious in what it preserves and what it leaves out. Demographic history is more univocal. Clearly we have to use documents of this kind, if that is all that exists. But we have to do so bearing in mind this warning; assessing emotional states is obviously an especially delicate, not to say dangerous, enterprise. For example Ariès, the founder of modern childhood history, concludes that the feelings of indifference about children in earlier cultures were 'not really very far removed from the callousness of the Roman or Chinese societies which practised the exposure of new-born children'.[14] Such callousness was 'only natural in the community conditions of the time', before the 'demographic revolution'. His idea smacks of advanced ethnocentricism; exposure may be a way of adjusting the number and sex of children to the resources of the *famiglia*. Or possibly of ridding oneself of illegitimate children. But as the politician and novelist Disraeli long ago observed such practices were no less common on the banks of the Thames than on those of the Ganges.

However there is concrete evidence of some movement in the study of tombstones in the Roman Empire which shows that over time there was an increase in the numbers celebrating children as compared with adults and in those commemorating women as compared with men.[15] These trends were strongest in the urban milieu where a new population of employed freedmen (presumably with no lineage ties) emphasised the elementary family of man, woman and children. Interestingly a similar progression has been found in American tombstones between 1660 and 1813.[16] The common factor is not the advent of Christianity but rather of urbanization. For in Rome the change was not as marked in the rural areas of North Africa nor in the mountainous areas of eastern France where lineage structures presumably continued to be important. No direct derivation is envisaged but similar economic forces are seen as producing similar results.[17] 'Roman-type behaviour' endured the longest in the urban centres of northern Italy and in the lowlands of north-western Europe along the corridor of the Rhine, that is where the 'small family household' is held to dominate.

The urban population consisted largely of small artisans, traders and others who worked in more individualistic ways. Other scholars too speak of the growth of individualism in Rome.[18] But that was also true of other urban centres where a much greater emphasis was placed on the lineage or extended kinship, as in India, China and in some urban situations in Italy. Surely the greater atomism of later Roman family life has to do with the fact that the population was heavily composed of freed slaves in these professions who by definition had been uprooted from their kinship networks, while the inhabitants of the newly emerging towns of the United States were cut off less radically but in a similar manner.

The simple nuclear family has been seen as the basis of residential and social arrangements generally and as we have observed, some have seen this feature as going back to later Rome. But complex families also existed and in Christian Europe these have arisen largely through the death of a spouse and by the subsequent remarriage of the survivor, creating new step-relationships ('in-laws' in an earlier terminology). In Rome however the numbers and complexity of complex families were greater because of divorce and subsequent remarriage.[19] Augustan legislation penalized men and women who did not remarry, although attitudes to the practice were ambivalent. So too they were under Christianity, but the balance swung decisively the other way. The Romans praised widows that never remarried as *univirae* (of one man). It has been suggested that while the Greeks encouraged the remarriage of widows, about 65 per cent of Athenian widows remained unmarried.

Close Marriages

In many ways the classical family provided the background against which Christianity reacted. I have argued that one important change and central to the new dispensation was the ban on marriages to close kin (including affinal and spiritual ones) who provided possible spouses not only for the Greeks and Romans but for much of Eurasia as well. In querying this argument, my proposition has been summarized in the following words: 'the Church's extension of the incest prohibition was responsible for a major change from endogamy to the exogamy characteristic of the medieval and modern period'.[20] Against this it is argued that 'endogamy, although legally permitted, was not normal in either a prescriptive or a behavioural sense before the fourth century'. To use the terms endogamy and exogamy in this context is misleading since anthropologists (who invented the terms) employ them in a specific sense of group prohibitions. Exogamy is the rule of marrying out, endogamy the rule of marrying within. What we are talking about in Rome is whether close marriage was permitted, not whether members of kin groups married in. Close marriages were clearly permitted in early Rome, just as they were in early Greece; even if not 'normal' in a statistical sense, it was not abnormal but rather acceptable. Indeed most significantly in Greece it was prescriptive in the case of heiresses, of *epiklerates*. With the coming of Christianity, close marriage was forbidden. True, not successfully forbidden in every case, but it was considered wrong, unacceptable – it meant one had to seek a dispensation (in rural Italy even in the 1970s, I found).[21] If one did not, the heirs could be declared illegitimate, a terrible weapon to put in the hands of one's enemies.

The criticism of my suggestion concerning the possibility of close marriage in Rome has been countered by the claim that it has taken insufficient account of prosopography, of biographical history.[22] However, while accepting the possibility of close marriage, it is denied that patrilateral parallel marriage (marriage to the father's brother's daughter) had anything to do with the preferential Arabian system of such unions.[23] Certainly it was not preferential in an overall way in Rome but close marriage between lineage members was possible and 'preferred' for similar purposes, for example, in making isogamous unions (between equals) to avoid misalliance. The fact that cousin marriages took place is clear from literature and from epitaphs.[24] Christian rulers on the other hand prohibited close marriage among kin, affines and spiritual kin. The contrast with Rome and Islam is clear. But such societies are not endogamous with regard to kin; as has been pointed out for Islam and for Rome, there may be advantages for some in distant marriages, in others for close ones.[25] Both options are open.

The contrast cannot be phrased in terms of exogamy and endogamy, only in terms of whether or not close marriages were allowed (not prescribed) and if I did not make it clear enough in denying the appropriateness of those terms, that was because historians were already using them in a confusing way.[26] But in both cases the system was and remained broadly endogamous regarding class. Not every marriage was class isogamous, since many were hypergamous (up for women) or hypogamous (down for women), but such unions are themselves indicative of the dominance of 'class' considerations.[27]

Close marriage between relatives, consanguineous or affinal, had two possible 'economic motives'. Marriages between cousins, attested within certain families in the late Republic, kept the property 'in the family'. Other cousin marriages avoided a misalliance for a woman with little dowry; that is, they maintained family status.[28] So, during the pagan period, marriage with first cousins was practised but not preferred let alone prescribed;[29] it rarely was in Eurasia as a whole but it remained an available family strategy.

One reason was that Roman marriage made allowance both for love and choice in the Republican as well as in Imperial periods.[30] In the latter period the state intruded to a greater extent than before into domestic affairs. The Julian law on adultery and fornication attempted to control sexual practices, leading to earlier and more frequent marriages and to more discretion in courtship. The Julian and Papio-Poppaean laws on intermarriage were examples of this outside intervention in family matters which led to a drop in the marriage age of senators, and put pressure on both participants and the institution.

Whatever the Roman situation regarding close marriage, it is quite clear from documents such as Gregory's letter to Augustine that in much of earlier Europe, just as in all that part of the Mediterranean not converted to Christianity, such unions were not only allowed but in some cases preferred. For centuries the favoured Islamic marriage has been with the father's brother's daughter, which was 'incestuous' by Christian standards. As I have remarked, it is not accidental that this is the marriage the Greeks prescribed for an heiress taking her parent's property since it kept the wealth within the family. In Ancient Israel, as the story of the daughters of Zelophahad relates, such women had to marry within the 'tribe'.

Regarding close marriage, it has been correctly noted (and this was precisely my point) that 'The narrower incest prohibitions of Roman law permitted wider choice of spouses than later canon law did'.[31] The author goes on to add, 'Nevertheless, as Plutarch noted, even before the establishment of Christianity Roman marriage tended to be more exogamous than in the eastern Mediterranean'. Given my definition of exogamy as a rule of marrying out, and it is the standard anthropological definition of a term introduced by lawyer-anthropologists, it is not easy to understand how one group can be 'more exogamous' than another. What the author possibly means is that the proportion of distant marriages was greater compared with close marriages. The co-existence of the two has been discussed for North Africa in a political context. Yet I would nevertheless describe Arab marriage as 'close' (since it permits, encourages, but does not prescribe, close unions between kin) and Christian marriage as 'distant' (rejecting close marriage) in quite concrete ways.

Closeness in this discussion has been confined to kin but there is another sense in which Eurasian societies (including Christian) encourage in-marriage in opposition to African ones, and that relates to marriage within the same social strata. An 'incest prohibition' of the kinship kind (instituting prohibited degrees) is quite consistent with the ideal of group (for example, class) endogamy, what the great French medievalist, Marc Bloch, called 'marriage in a circle', and it is at the latter level that there is a stark contrast between (most of) Africa and (most of) Eurasia, as we see for example in the figures on marriage among the Gonja of West Africa where there is no tendency (in thought or in actuality) to confine marriages within a single social group. On this 'class' (or preferably 'estate') level, Roman and Greek societies were in-marrying, even endogamous.

The ban on close marriage was not of course the only change introduced by Christianity. Going once again counter to both its Hebrew and its Roman backgrounds, the Church prohibited divorce. The reasons for this are not entirely clear. The argument that 'whomsoever God hath brought together, let no man set asunder', that is, marriage is a sacrament, blessed by God, could as well be applied to Hebrew marriage, yet there a bill of divorcement was possible. Men at least could seek for divorce. The prohibition was perhaps linked to the establishment of a new sect, with the idea that one should marry within the (Christian) community and permanently (lest you stray outside). One of the effects however was certainly to restrict strategies of heirship, since in a monogamous society divorcing a barren wife in favour of another was an important way of seeking an heir, as witness the extravagant marital career of Henry VIII. There was certainly a decisive breach with earlier European custom, establishing a pattern which continues to influence marriage to this day.

Christian Influence

The influence of Christian ideology and practice on late Roman society had made its mark by the end of the fourth century.[32] Change gathered momentum in the patristic period before the establishment of the Ostrogothic kingdom in Italy in the sixth century which was the beginning of a period of a 'rather tense relationship' with the church lasting until the advent of the Carolingians. This is the very period that saw the great build-up of church lands in Gaul and elsewhere, establishing the church as an organization complementary to but also competing with the state.

The significance of the changes in kinship and marriage beginning in Late Antiquity and linked with the coming of Christianity have been recognized by some other classicists. The ability of Romans to 'construct their families' through adoption and close marriage is said to have given way to a 'profound rupture' between classical Rome and later ages. 'Rome enjoyed a large degree of liberty to create their kinship groups . . . and to choose their heirs' (through testaments).[33] There was no 'impossible marriage', and divorce and remarriage were both available with adoption as ways of building families. All of these were possibilities that 'the Church took away from their descendants in Europe and that modern states have not reinstated'.[34] In many cases they now have, after a series of struggles, but the problem is why did these changes occur in the first place?

Roman practice 'allowed more flexibility in constructing kinship than did later European societies. A man could break the link with a son through emancipation and create one through adoption; he could replace or add one set of affines for another through divorce and remarriage. The narrower incest prohibitions permitted a wider choice of spouse than did later canon law; close cousins were potential spouses, as were the spouses of older siblings. These are precisely the differences to which I earlier called attention in discussing the role of the Christian church, namely in adoption, divorce and closer marriage.[35] For me the major problem was why these features changed when there was no warrant for the new dispensation either in Roman law or in Hebrew scriptures. And they were promulgated before there was any major social shift, for example, in the mode of production. That question is the subject of the next chapter.

3

The Coming of Christianity

The coming of Christianity radically changed the European family in many major respects. Some historians have claimed those changes related to the increased stress on the conjugal family, which some Romanists have seen as developing in the empire and other historians in Carolingian times.[1] Others have seen a parallel development of 'individualism' under Christianity while yet others have attributed this supposed characteristic to German influence.[2] However while it can be argued that the devaluation of the Roman gens and the bilateral organization of the Germanic tribes may have encouraged such tendencies, these features all seem more widely embedded in human society. So I choose to look at more precise differences with earlier Europe, either classical or 'tribal', especially as evidenced in the efforts of Christian missionaries to change the practices of their converts.

Prohibited Marriages

Firstly, the Church brought in new rules for marriage that transformed existing ones. They forbad marriage to close kin, not only consanguines but also affinal relatives and later spiritual ones traced through godparenthood, a system which the church itself invented or elaborated to provide its own ecclesiastical equivalent of family ties. The prohibited degrees as Europe later knew them seem to have begun with the ban on marriage to a husband's brother (the levirate) in Canon 2 of the Council of Neocaesaria (314). Then, in the East in the late fourth century, ordination was denied to those men who had married a dead wife's sister (the sororate) or a brother's daughter. Wider restrictions were worked out in the Gallic councils of the sixth and seventh centuries against some heavy opposition and these were further extended by a council of Pope Gregory II held at Rome about 721 which seemed to exclude marriage to any relative whatsoever.[3] That same council also initiated the ban on marriage to spiritual kin.

Those prohibitions, which changed in range over time, ran directly against the practices both of the Holy Book (Judaic law permitted and even encouraged marriage to close kin) and of Roman law, which varied over time but also generally permitted close marriages, as did the major Eurasian societies.[4] Such close marriages had been permitted, though not prescribed, in other parts of the classical world. Early Greece had allowed the marriage even of half-siblings while an heiress or *epiklerate*, a daughter who inherited in the absence of brothers, was expected to marry her father's brother's son, the preferred marriage in Arab societies and later common throughout the eastern and southern Mediterranean. It was equally the case in Judaism that an heiress was forbidden to marry outside the patrilineal clan; in both instances the property had to be retained within it by in-marriage.

The changes that Christianity made are clear from the pronouncements of the Christian missionaries to the 'pagans' when they tried to combat earlier practices and apply the new. For example the first archbishop of Canterbury, Saint Augustine, asked Pope Gregory in Rome for instruction as to what he should do about the unions of those converting to Christianity. The Pope's reply was circulated in much of western Europe, providing a guide to the problems arising out of applying the rules of the new dispensation. Essentially these instructions had to do with the prohibition on close marriages. Henceforth it was necessary to marry outside the range of immediate kin, and that included affines so that not only the levirate but also the sororate and cousin marriages were forbidden.

Close kinship marriages can be seen as consolidating the wider relationships between kin, especially within kin groups. The church was concerned to weaken these wider ties, whether of clanship or of kinship, lest they threaten its increasing control of the population and its power to acquire bequests from them. Marrying cousins and other kin can do both of these, for it can keep family and property firmly together rather than dispersing ties and goods more widely.

So the church actively discouraged such marriages, quite contrary to earlier practice which permitted them, they were now condemned as *incasta*, incestuous. This shift is made clear in the account of the life of Saint Aubin or Albin who was born in the region of Vannes (Morbihan, in Western Gaul) in 469 and died there in 550. According to the Saint's life, many lords of the area at this period married their sister or their daughter. At a time when the bishops kept quiet out of fear for what it might cost them, Aubin did not cease to object to this practice. 'You will see that they'll have my head and I'll finish up like John the Baptist', he used to say. His prediction did not come true. In the end he forced the Church of Gaul to condemn these marriages and to excommunicate all those who contracted them.

The reference here is probably not to marrying full sisters and actual daughters but to 'classificatory' ones, to those included in the same verbal category (since as far as we know marriage to the former was confined to a few areas of the Near East and to the latter not attested at all). But what the document indicates is that the Christian Church was in the business of imposing specific norms of domestic behaviour on its converts, in this case a ban on close marriages (except by obtaining a dispensation or much later by becoming a 'heretic' or a Protestant). Not only were these marriages effectively forbidden but at the same time notions of incest underwent a radical change. Contrary to much common opinion, there is no universal ban on sexual relations between brothers and sisters; at certain times half-siblings were allowed to marry in Ancient Israel, Ancient Greece, elsewhere in the Middle East, and most notably in Ancient Egypt where marriage even between full siblings was not only allowed but in some circumstances preferred.[5] Christianity changed all that with its insistence on more distant marriages, seeing intercourse within the prohibited degrees as being 'unchaste'.

Godparenthood

That notion applied not only to consanguineal kin but to affines (those related by marriage) and to those related through godparenthood. Spiritual kinship, godparenthood, is often treated as a form of 'ritual kinship' of which there are frequent examples (such as blood brotherhood) in other parts of the world. But in its Christian form it was a specific invention of the church which had wide-ranging effects. In the first place it provided for guarantors and guardians of the spiritual faith of the growing child. In any developing church, in any conversion situation, the problem of apostasy must always be present; through remarriage or for other reasons a parent might relapse into the earlier religion, so leading the children to do likewise. Godparents inhibited any such move on the part of children and possibly of adults; especially in the shape of 'fairy godmothers' (the opposite of the 'wicked uncle' or stepfather), they kept their charges on the straight and narrow. Secondly, godparents provided a set of ties that were explicitly 'kinship' ('parenthood') yet had been created by baptism, through entry into the church. Those ties were endowed with a strength similar to consanguinity, since godparents named children, looked after their spiritual welfare, and came within the prohibited degrees for marriage. It is they who are essential at a Christian baptism, not the parents themselves. Their later dominance in South America was partly due to the fact that after conversion such ties could be imposed as an addition to indigenous forms of kinship and marriage, reshaping them in the image of the church. At the same time existing ties were inevitably weakened by the presence of a powerful alternative frame of reference. It was Christ's intention to deconstruct the traditional family to establish new norms and to that aim godparenthood made a substantial contribution.

Church and Women

In this process the church in effect threw its weight against the existence of strong kin groups, especially patrilineal clans or lineages. Such groups might threaten the work of the church, and in particular the accumulation of funds; it preferred 'an undifferentiated kinship system, of a cognatic group conforming to the teachings of the church' as against the agnatic groupings that existed in ancient Rome and seem to have had a partial rebirth after the High Middle Ages. That preference was particularly reflected in the notions of many women, as in the 'gendered' genealogy prompted by Mona Gemma in fourteenth-century Florence.[6] Indeed the church systematically favoured the tracing of kinship through women (as well as men) from whom they recruited the bulk of their congregations and their resources. Women lived longer than men and through the dowry (at marriage) and the dower (from their dead husband's estate), the well-off among them could control a significant segment of the wealth of a community.

Such a trend was also apparent in the church's views on conjugal relationships between the partners. Its regulations on marriage have been described as 'extremely liberal' and from the sixteenth century matrimony had to be the result of the free will ('love') of the contracting parties and even clandestine marriages 'without the benefit of clergy' were considered valid. That tendency was manifest much earlier. For centuries the church had been fighting secular conceptions of marriage.

The Church and Property

The church's close interest in the family has been accounted for in a number of ways. The suggested connections with over-arching ideologies of an ethical or moral kind appear to be largely post facto (though their consequences were important) and fail to take account of deep-seated contradictions (for example, that the New Testament came out against family ties). There are more proximate reasons for this interest. It has been argued that this 'had nothing to do with questions of succession but instead had the aim of imposing its control on a moment of such importance in the life of the faithful'.[7] Control was certainly one reason as we have seen. Putting the events of birth, marriage and death in priestly hands gave the church immense power which was represented by the priest and church located in every parish under the charge of the bishop. Perhaps no other world religion has had quite such a formidable apparatus of local control, related to its successful missionary activity.

Another had to do with the considerable benefits, spiritual as well as material, which the church could gain from such control, which in turn freed couples (especially women) from parental authority. The story of Romeo and Juliet draws attention to the conflict between the aims of kingroups and those of the church. As has been remarked, in recognizing free choice, the church 'objectively favoured women', a fact that women explored.[8] All religious activity necessarily involves gifts from mankind to the gods (through their representatives on earth) in the form of offerings, sacrifice, prayer, art and ritual. Gifts to the gods require an alienation (a 'sacrifice') from the individual or from the family, as is the case with all charity to whomever directed. Of course there are concomitant rewards and reciprocities but by and large charity involves the giving of material goods in return for spiritual benefits. The church depended upon such gifts to establish itself as a 'great organization', for the build-up and maintenance of its plant, its personel and its manifold activities, scholarly, charitable and sacerdotal.

The Christian church started out with nothing, indeed it was committed to poverty. Gradually it acquired responsibilities (towards its widows, for example), personnel and places of assembly, all of which needed material support, especially after the conversion of Constantine (312 CE) and the assumption of an official role. Widows were an interesting case. The earlier practice whereby they were automatically eligible to be taken in a further (leviratic) marriage or quasi-marriage by their affinal kin, the brothers of their dead husbands, was now forbidden, though it had been widespread in the Mediterranean. One possible reason for the ban was that the church wanted to look after its own whereas the levirate meant that widow and children might come under the care of a non-Christian husband; there was no possibility of choosing (by 'freewill') one of the right kind, now no longer defined by kinship alone. Moreover rich, unmarried widows were likely to contribute more effectively to the church than married ones, especially by leaving bequests and engaging in church-oriented activities. At the same time poor widows (less rewarding as brides) now had to be looked after by the church, a fact that provided a specific reason for soliciting bequests.

Of the contrast with the public, municipal gifts of pagan Roman testaments, it has been said: 'What was new about Christian testamentary giving was its orientation towards the future life and its focus on monastic houses, as well as the disadvantaged, widows, and the poor'.[9] Such gifts, 'redefined relationships among close kin', a portion going to the Church who administered charity and organized prayer. For 'alms extinguished sin'.

Such bequests were encouraged in other ways that also involved changes in the system of kinship and marriage. Throughout Eurasia, families were able to continue their line and in many cases their estate by a number of 'strategies of heirship', which included adoption, plural marriage (or concubinage), divorce (of a barren spouse) and remarriage, and in certain instances by close marriage itself. The extent of these practices is indicated by a number of learned articles, on divorce in Old Testament times, on 'Adoption as a remedy for infertility in the period of the patriarchs', on polygamy, and on 'l'obligation de mariage dans un degré rapproché'. For Rome there are studies on divorce[10] and adoption, on remarriage, and on close marriage.

Adoption

Adoption is an obvious way of recruiting an heir when there are no children, or none of the relevant sex, and to that practice I will return.

Concubinage

Plural marriage may be motivated by considerations of sexual attraction or the need for additional domestic assistance, but one major factor in Eurasian societies is the desire to have children when the existing spouse is barren or cannot produce an heir of the right sex. That same result can be achieved by those forms of concubinage that provide legitimate offspring. Concubinage was common throughout Europe and Asia. Abraham, for example, bred heirs and offspring with the aid of his wife's 'handmaid'. The Christian church appears initially to have been ambiguous about such arrangements, especially in relation to the clergy. In the western branch priests were meant to be celibate; they were to have no interest in progeny or ultimately in property. Nevertheless clerical concubinage was common until after the Gregorian reforms of the eleventh century. But in general such arrangements were disapproved of, one reason for which, I argue, was that the church benefited from confining inheritance to the true heirs, or even in not having heirs at all. Hence it prohibited practices that provided alternative candidates.

Disputing this view of concubinage, which was a possible strategy in Ancient Israel enshrined in Holy Writ, a Roman historian queries whether the church really managed to alter the practice of taking concubines, 'but if it did suppress concubinage the effect would have been to increase the supply of legitimate heirs and to decrease the flow of property to the Church . . . . Overall, it would seem that the principal argument of the earlier book

[Goody 1983] is in some respects vitiated by the methodological statements and descriptions of Roman practice in the later book' (Goody 1990).[11] There can be no question that the elimination of concubinage was long part of the church's programme, only fulfilled perhaps with the Gregorian reforms and subsequently with the Counter-Reformation; even later there remained some doubts. But as for its elimination increasing the number of legitimate heirs, that argument is unsustainable. In those Near Eastern societies that allow concubinage or plural marriage, these unions are often entered into when the first wife is barren. If these practices ceased to exist, there would be no legitimate heirs at all. The bed of the second wife or concubine was an addition, not an alternative. Even where concubinage does not have this function, as in harem conditions, there is no evidence at all that it reduces the number of a man's progeny, though it may reduce the fertility of the individual women. Regarding his wider remarks, the author has I think misunderstood the problem behind my earlier book, which was not simply to suggest ways in which the church had modified Roman law but in which it had rejected certain practices enshrined in its own Holy Scriptures, such as the levirate or concubinage. Indeed the study began with the problem of the divergences between the two sides of the Mediterranean and touched upon the contrast with Islam as well as with Rome and Israel.

Divorce

The argument concerning the church's actions restricting heirship is true of the ban not so much on divorce as on subsequent re-marriage. Once again we come across an institution that was widespread, though not universal, in Eurasia and was certainly prominent in the Mediterranean, in Judaism, in Rome as it later was in Islam. Yet it was deliberately banned by the Christian church, though not immediately, in a way that structured interpersonal relations in Europe until well into the twentieth century. Julian the Apostate had allowed women the possibility even of initiating divorce. In the early 380s that option was deplored by a Roman priest, Ambrosiaster, who stressed that women should be submissive to men in general and to bishops in particular.

The Christian resistance to divorce possibly played a part in Constantine's constitution of 331 which restricted the dissolution of unions. A year later Theodosius pointed out that for the good of the children it should not be easy to dissolve a marriage. But civil law was reluctant to go further and Christian communities themselves had to try to discourage divorce among their own members.[12]

Remarriage

One of the problems about any remarriage was explicitly pointed out by Tertullian; widows might marry pagan husbands (2.1.4.). Tertullian, of course, was an extremist; others among the early Fathers of the Church allowed younger widows to remarry, thinking that the safest course to take. But there were strong counter-currents. For widowers too should remain unmarried, possibly choosing one or more *spiritual* wives among the widows. Quite the opposite pressures existed in Rome; as the result of Augustus, women had had to pay a penalty if they did not marry. Why did this change take place? We find later ideological justifications in terms of preserving the family. But which family? And did it maintain anything, since the ban was on remarriage after divorce rather than on the separation itself. That prohibition meant one could have no legitimate heirs other than those by the first wife, yet in other regions the search for an heir was an important aim of divorce or at least of additional marriage or subsequent remarriage. Remarriage as we have seen might permit the former partners to establish new relationships with non-Christians, endangering the religious affiliations of the children as well. But it also meant the possibility of producing more children (especially when there had been none before) and that intervention endangered the likelihood of bequests to the church.

Heirship

The same is true of adoption, another strategy of heirship that was again widespread in Eurasia but forbidden by the Christian church. This prohibition also lasted until the present century in Europe (the nineteenth in the United States). On the subject of adoption we have a quite explicit statement of Christian objections. Salvianus, a fifth-century Bishop of Marseilles, explains that all man's worldly goods come to him from God and to God they should return. While it was permissible to make an exception for one's own children, that was not true for any collateral or fictional heirs. Indeed he refers to adopted children as 'children of perjury', cheating God (or his church) of what was rightfully his. This statement makes it quite clear why the institution should be banned, in the interests of the church and of spirituality. The confrontation with past practice is very explicit and had an enormous influence on the future; even if there were a few exceptions later on, the ban was largely complied with throughout Christendom over the centuries.

The radical changes that Christianity brought about in European kinship turn on the fact that the church is included as an heir.[13] The church 'joined the family', a situation which also made it the focus of sibling rivalry and family jealousies. In 321 Constantine had declared that testators were free to bequeath whatever they wished to the church. But subsequent legislation in 370 already attempted to prevent widows and wards from making bequests to legacy-hunting clerics, thereby disappointing the expectations of their next of kin.

The church also created its own brand of spiritual kinship by means of baptismal sponsorship. The new 'kinsfolk' became referred to by kinship terms, *compater* being introduced in the seventh century.[14] The resulting obligations and prohibitions, (which included the prohibition on marriage) 'have characterized European Catholic societies and their missionary descendants over-seas until the nineteenth century and after'.[15]

The practical results of all these changes on the distribution of wealth by inheritance can be seen in the extraordinary alteration in the Church's material circumstances. In Gaul between the fifth and the eighth centuries the church acquired rights to over one-third of all the arable land of the kingdom. All this land had in effect to come from family holdings. Some came by gift, some by inheritance; the church claimed a proportion of every will, the soul's part, but in other cases much more, especially when a couple had no direct heirs, that is, in roughly 20 per cent of the cases. Church regulations limited the possible strategies of heirship and it benefited thereby to an enormous extent.

Domestic Life

Extensive claims have been made for the influence of Christianity on domestic relationships. I have discussed, somewhat sceptically, assertions that have been made about increased stress on the elementary or nuclear family, on individualism, on love. Each of these claims contains some element of truth but they have also been made for the later Roman period. In my view the assertions have to be interpreted at a more specific, more concrete level, in terms of variables such as those I have just discussed. Otherwise one enters into a disputed area of vagueness and uncertainty. For example, according to one author, 'Christianity instituted a new era not only in the history of monasticism but also in the history of feminism.'[16] She sees women as being accepted as 'fully equal to men in their spiritual potential and being able to transcend sex roles'. Certainly that trend did not begin with the suffragettes, with Mary Wollstonecraft, nor yet with the Renaissance. It is not 'modern'. But such broad claims to originality are exaggerated and indicate once again the propensity of the Christian West to make unjustifiable claims to priority, here about monasticism and women. Regarding monasteries, in Hindu India hermits lived in groups (*ashrams*) from about 6000 BCE but it was Jainism that probably had the earliest organized monastic life. The founder, Mahavira, gathered some of his followers into groups of monks and nuns, though later one sect, the Digambaras, disallowed the latter. But in general they were rootless celibates, who moved from one temporary resting place to another. In Buddhism monasteries as well as monasticism became very important, though again there were few nuns.

Women

Regarding women, one needs to look in more detail at the different aspects of women's life that were affected. What I have called diverging devolution, associated with the women's property complex, existed throughout the major societies of Eurasia. Women were largely but not entirely excluded from religious, political and some economic activities under Christianity as much as elsewhere, whatever the ideology; on the other hand because they too inherited or were endowed with property like their brothers, they were especially valued by the church as potential contributors to its good works. But that was also the case with Buddhism and Jainism, since this form of devolution characterized all the major Eurasian civilizations.

With regard to the family, it has been claimed that women benefited from the ban on divorce, insisted on by the church. But such a ban may have been unfavourable to those seeking to free themselves from an oppressive or abusive husband and it is significant that when divorce was allowed in the French Revolution, women constituted the majority of the petitioners (as is the case today). And in England and America, women in the nineteenth century led the campaign in its favour. In any case the Christian ban was accompanied by an insistence on obedience.

Older women in particular have been seen as beneficiaries of Christianity, which it has been argued brought about a revolution in the traditional system of values in their regard; previously old women were scorned, now they were cherished.[17] In fact rich women had always been prized while poorer women were rarely undervalued in their own families. What now happened was that the church attempted to attract both, some as givers, the others as receivers.

Women and Wealth

Women clearly played a great part in the the life of the church. They constituted a large majority of early Christians and spread the word to other women in ways that men could not;[18] Manichaean and other women did the same. They were perhaps attracted by the charity of the church but the wealthy also participated and were encouraged to do so by the clerics. So women became the spearheads in the transformation of domestic structures that Christianity brought about, even if it was the male clerics who in the end benefited most obviously from their generous contributions of a material kind. Any imbalance between the numbers of male and female members was a feature of a religion of conversion; obviously in an established religion the numbers of adherents are roughly equal, even if their zeal as practitioners is not, for women remained the main followers of the faith, especially widows who were no longer automatically married off to their dead husband's kin but devoted themselves to good works and to charity.[19]

Indeed widows were no longer required to remarry at all, but men often tried to force them to do so. As a result in the fourth century emperors like Constantine, Jovian and Theodosius took strong measures to prevent such unions happening.[20] Nevertheless some did remarry; a wealthy widow might marry a socially inferior husband who would thus be quite dependent upon her.[21] Others who remained unmarried were often visited by clergy who stretched out their hands not to bless but to receive. Again, counter measures were taken. 'In an edict which was read out in the churches of Rome on 30 July 370, the emperors decided that clerics were forbidden to visit the house of widows', nor were they allowed to receive gifts or legacies, though this restriction did not prevent the church benefiting from bequests, always at the expense of the close kin. Unmarried widows 'frequently used their fortune for the benefit of the church and the poor, and thus injured the financial interests of their own aristocratic families. Fabiola built a guest-house for travellers in Ostia (Ep. 77.10); Paula spent so much money on the poor and on a monastery in Bethlehem that she robbed her own children of their inheritance and, instead, left them with large debts (Ep. 108); Furia was encouraged by Jerome to give all her possessions to the Lord (Ep. 54), and Marcella would have given everything she had to the poor if her mother had not objected (Ep. 107)'.[22] Other widows supported important clerics. 'In a way these wealthy widows had taken over the role of the male aristo-crats, who had always been accustomed to establish and consolidate their positions within the ancient cities by making gifts and initiating large building projects. In contrast to this male ener-getism, these widows directed their attention to the poor and monks. They did not build baths, temples or theatres, but monas-teries and guesthouses for the poor; these activities, however, subverted the family fortunes of the high aristocrats and, not surprisingly, the emperors attempted to protect their political supporters against the erosion of their fortunes by means of edicts'.[23] It was the church that guided this shift, both from fami-lies and from municipalities.

In this way a great deal of wealth was alienated from families to the church. Whereas previously such wealth had been given to support the municipalities, there was no longer money coming in to keep up the baths and theatres.[24] The towns decayed, the churches flourished. A paradigmatic case is that of Verulamium, a major city in Roman Britain, which fell into decay in the fourth century. Its theatre, its hypocaust, its forum, its walls, all fell into ruin. The local wealth, as well as the bricks themselves, went to build the great Abbey complex that grew up around the Romanesque church. But the Church did not simply replace the town as the recipient of aristocratic wealth; it greatly extended its net by encouraging changes in the family that would alter the patterns of heirship, so that it profited to a much greater extent from the alienation of family wealth, as we see from the fact that it built up vast landholdings, extensive buildings, and a large staff in the course of a few centuries. The beginning of the accumulation of land in Gaul corresponded to the great development of monastic communities at the end of the fourth century.[25] This development gave rise to the Rule of Saint Benedict, but Italian monasticism passed into northern Europe only in the seventh century.

It was the City of God, not the city on earth, that interested the church; the laws of God were preferred to those of the Roman State.[26] 'Christian preoccupation with moral and religious issues converged with an existing tradition of imperial intervention in details of daily urban life.' It was at baptism that a person born into the terrestrial city was reborn and *adopted* into the City of God.[27]

Shift of Resources

The shift of resources to the church was radical. An account of Italy in the early Middle Ages explains how the country reverted to 'aboriginal circumstances' in the seventh and eighth centuries, leaving a vacuum which the church was well equipped to exploit. In Italy this exploitation took the form of Carolingian monastic imperialism, the building of great ecclesiastical complexes some-times on earlier Roman estate centres. Carolingian domination established the Gregorian chant, literacy and its own iconology. Artisans were drawn within the complex, becoming servants of the monastery. There the great benefactors were entertained and later buried. The monastery was a major focus of commercial activity, receiving investments and returning tribute.[28]

The reasons I have suggested for the changes in the domestic order, such as the prohibitions on close marriage, have been described as 'economic', in opposition to which Christian notions of purity (against incest) have been proposed. But there is no con-tradiction. The reasons are not simply 'economic' unless one regards the building of churches to the glory of God, the estab-lishment of monastic institutions and the support of the needy as economic in any limiting sense. Clearly they are also ideological and religious, but like much religious activity they have economic implications. Regarding Christian notions of purity, these applied to all sexual intercourse, not simply to close marriage. There is nothing in itself less pure about marrying a cousin than marrying an outsider; it was sex that was impure. Incest (*incasta*) was a way of categorizing prohibited marriages and one should not be distracted by late nineteenth-century discussions, psychological and sociological, about the topic with their claims to universality and possibly to innateness and degeneracy.

Sexuality

However sexuality and in that sense purity was another focus of attention in the Christian church. According to one author, 'the place occupied by sexuality in the life of late Antiquity changed considerably due to the rise of asceticism and the increasingly negative attitude of the Christian clergy towards the body'.[29] The 'admired few' renounced sexuality, while the congregation opted for a restrained practice. Of course such renunciation occurred in other world religions such as Buddhism and Jainism that adopted monasticism. Moreover, even in Europe this trend is rightly seen as starting earlier, in Hellenistic times. And we have to insist that the admired few did not always set the tone for the rest of society. All societies place some restrictions on sexual intercourse; in the world religions there are often specialists who remain celibate and pure. But this element can never be more than a respected minority while the bulk of the population get on with the business of copulation and reproduction, for themselves and for society. Although among the Cathars the Perfects gave up sex, we know from Montaillou and other sources that their followers behaved like normal human beings. That was also the case within orthodox Christianity. While the penitentials decreed punishment for lapses from the rules, there were no sanctions against sleeping with one's wife or with one's husband.

Resistance

The fact that a divorce existed between those who were expected to apply certain norms, such as celibacy, and the bulk of the population, raises the question of the degree to which views of the body for example did mark the culture as a whole or how far the priests were performing a role on behalf of and in opposition to the rest. It also raised the further question of how far other norms, which I have suggested often ran contrary to family interests, were in fact obeyed or applied. Firstly, there was the possibility open to the rich of purchasing exemption through a dispensation or to the powerful

of just ignoring such injunctions. Secondly, the rules could be lifted
if the marriage pool was small or if a woman could not raise the
money for a fitting dowry. Or if the woman was over twenty-five
or the man was a widower with young children. In these cases
dowry could be kept among the kin.[30] It is suggested that regarding
my thesis concerning changes introduced by the church to the legal
rules relating to inheritance strategies, to assess the disruption of
traditional life, we need to look at practice as well as codes.[31] That
of course is true and the basis of much anthropological work. A
significant part of my argument was that the norms (whether legal
or not) introduced by the church went against the best interests of
families, hence the resistance at various times and levels. Many of
the sources stress the role of codes, but my evidence was certainly
not limited to these. Wills, for example, are instructions for the
disposition of property and if they reflect codes, that is an indication of the power (of state or church) that lies behind them. Secular
state law is after all backed by a monopoly of force and if it is not
the only regulator, as anthropologists are the first to agree, it is
nevertheless an important one, at least for certain classes and for
certain events. Regarding adoption, for example, Roman historians
may find problematic the question of why it was not used more
often in the late Republic and Empire, but a qualitative difference
occurred when the priest Salvianus declared adoptees to be
cheating God of his due. And the continuing absence of adoption,
which is after all a formal, public, legal status, had profound practical effects and has been linked, among other things, with the
numbers of abandoned children in parts of Europe after the
Counter-Reformation.[32] It was not possible to put illegitimate children out for adoption until this century; they had to be looked after
by other means which did not always provide the same kind of care
and commitment.

Law and Practice

In reviewing the discussions by historians and anthropologists
about the Roman family, the same author claims that they have
generally put too much emphasis on the law and have not allowed
enough for practice. For example he tends to play down the legal
rights of masters over female slaves, quoting an objection by a Stoic
philosopher to this abuse of one's authority for sexual purposes.
However objections are not the same thing as rights, and practice

is always the outcome of a struggle between the opposing forces. Equally, with regard to the exercise of paternal authority in marriage, he allows that 'canon law shifted the emphasis to consent between the spouses for a valid marriage, but underlying the formal change was a continuing tension between parent's insistence on the right of approval and their children's independence . . .'.[33] That of course is true; everyone has views on the marriage of their children. But his statement does not give sufficient weight to a change which could affect the legitimacy of children and their entitlement to inherit. It also overlooks the force of the disputes that arose when secular and religious rules came down on different sides, as in the conflicts over the decisions of the Council of Trent concerning parental consent, or in literary terms that between family duties and individual desires, the latter often supported by the church.

The Impact of Christianity in Mexico

It is difficult to assess the impact of Christianity on the family structures of the non-literate peoples of Europe from the documents that are available since these are basically of ecclesiastical origin or marked by theological debates, as in the works of Bede, Gregory of Tours and others. The collections of laws are influenced by Rome or Christianity or both, while the epics and sagas were all written down after the change in religion. Some insights into earlier practices can be gained when mention is made of pagan custom or of the backsliding of congregations, but the strength of the resistance is not easy to measure. However in conclusion, we may get some idea from accounts of the next great wave of conversion to Christianity, that on the American continent following the Spanish and Portuguese conquests. A recent account of the influence of the church on aspects of family structures emphasizes the intrusiveness of the missionary effort.

Soon after the conquest of Mexico, in the 1520s and 1530s the Church started to inculcate the Christian marriage ethic and conjugal life. The clergy reflected on local practice, consulted widely and then began to apply a 'unique and uniform code, valid everywhere, whatever the ethnic people or social status involved, and founded on a written tradition and law'. Some of these prescriptions, the primacy of reproduction, the condemnation of abortion and homosexuality, the protection of the marriage bond and the opprobrium heaped on adulterers, these prescriptions fitted with existing norms.[34] But as far as marriage regulations were concerned, there was a great problem with the autochthons.

The Church was attacking head-on the prerogatives of ancient ruling groups and communities, claiming sole jurisdiction over the rites of passage that marked out the life-cycle, the rituals of birth, marriage and death. It condemned polygyny (often replaced by concubinage), reducing every man to one wife; it established marriage prohibitions and turned marriage into a private affair, 'voluntary and not forced'. The nuclear family was stressed 'to the detriment of its domestic and social extensions', while the Spanish crown promoted the break-up of the wider family by its taxation policy. 'In the long term, the introduction of private property and the practice of making wills, together with the spread of a salaried class, contributed . . . to the emergence of a Western type of individualism and privatisation of social relations parallel to what the Church was advocating'[35]

The church also introduced its own conception of sexuality, 'claiming strict control over desire or pleasure'.[36] But its claims were often resisted, by the deliberate strategies of the inhabitants and by their resort to practices such as concubinage, bigamy and prostitution. As in Europe the insistence on monogamy eliminated the status of co-spouse who was reduced to being a concubine. It is possible that indissoluble marriage contributed to intensify the bond between mother and child, and emphasized the small nuclear family. But a dead mother could be substituted only by the step-mother who could never be a sister of the mother but had to be an outsider. This intrusion of Christianity on the American continent paralleled its intrusion into Europe and the effects must have been very similar.

4

The German Lands

How far did the German heritage influence the European family? On this topic there is much disagreement partly because little is known of practice while the sources on early Germanic law are difficult to interpret and much influenced by the interests of the classical authors making the comments. By the time the Germans are producing their own written laws, their society is being affected not only by Rome but also by Christianity and these factors have to be taken into account when trying to assess the state of affairs. It is for that reason that I have considered the German evidence after looking not only at Greece and Rome, but at Christianity too.

The German and other 'barbarian' peoples had no systems of writing (except for rudimentary 'runes') before intensive contact with the classical civilizations and then what remains of their self-generated writings consisted largely of formal legal codes. The archaeological record provides us with information about house types, material culture and settlement pattern, indicating some differentiation of access to resources and a variety of social environments varying from isolated houses to hamlets to nucleated villages. But so far as data on kinship (marriage and the family) are concerned, we have little except the comments of Roman writers like Tacitus, who often seem to be dealing in ideal types partly out of ignorance, partly to make political points about Roman life. It would of course be possible to make some guesses based on comparative ethnological material from more

recent times but that is dangerous and potentially almost as misleading as many of the speculative reconstructions of later
scholars working on that period.

Patrilineal or Bilateral?

Traditional scholarship often saw the early Germans and indeed
the Indo-Europeans as a whole as being characterized by agnatic
kinship structures and this trend has been supported by the use of
linguistic evidence (by Benveniste, for example) concerning terms
and groupings. The attempted reconstructions of early German
kinship by legal historians seem vague and improbable, like no
well-documented society we know of.[1] The Sippe is regarded as a
clan, though it is also suggested it was a neighbourhood group; the
concept of the family is seen as developing from a household
(including slaves) to a kin group; the father's complete authority is
stressed, while references are made to an earlier matrilineal organization on a highly speculative basis.

The patrilineal thesis was given much attention in Germany and
elsewhere. An alternative theory, upheld by Engels and going back
to Bachofen and to Morgan's *Ancient Society* (1877), has found
traces of early matriliny. The evidence for the latter is thoroughly
mistaken: It has been suggested that the close ties with a mother's
brother mean that at one time the Germanic clans may have been
matrilineal.[2] They do nothing of the sort. Most patrilineal and
cognatic societies allocate a special role to the maternal uncle. From
the time one has any evidence about the Germans, inheritance was
determinately agnatic, going first to children, then to brothers and
'uncles'. That was to change with Christianity. The former claim is
equally thin, a certain agnatic bias being taken as a survival of patrilineal clanship.

More realistically, other authors have emphasized the significance of bilateral (cognatic) relationships among the
Anglo-Saxons, not resulting from a purported breakdown of the
unilineal system but as the earliest known form of social organization among these peoples.[3] It has been shown that the Sippe was
not unilineal, although unilineal groups were more in evidence on
the Celtic fringes of Europe, such as Ireland and Scotland and in
some other marginal areas.[4] Discussion of the Sippe, attributions
of matrifocality,[5] talk of the dowry as wife purchase,[6] the prominent role of the mother's brother, all these features have been

misinterpreted to fit in with unwarrantedly speculative developmental schemes that have very little basis in reality; by and large discussions of early German kinship have dealt with 'imagined communities'.

The fact is that virtually no patrilineal system fails to recognize maternal ties; regarding neighbourhood, there is always some equivocation in the use of kinship concepts in their incorporation of co-residents as kin ('he is a member of the family') whether in the Tallensi (Ghana) *yir* or the Nuer (Southern Sudan) *thok dwiel*. What seems to stand out is that the Sippe was not unilineal and that kinship organization was based upon the kindred. The use of the term clan, by which most authorities refer to a unilineal group, is therefore misleading, except possibly for the patronymic groups that one appears to find in the fringe areas referred to above.

Bilateral kinship systems were widespread in early Germanic Europe and constituted for example 'the very core of Merovingian power structure'.[7] Brothers and sisters tended to marry in the same circle, but women were not simply pawns in these interfamilial alliances. Marriages of Frankish men to Gallo-Roman women led to the conversion of the former to Christianity and secured them ascendency in royal administration and in the church. Ties were important through both sides (bilaterally), through both men and women.

Size of Household

Another major discussion concerns a supposed change from larger to smaller households (sometimes spoken of as 'families'). It has been claimed that it was under the Carolingians that there occurred 'a shift from the extended family to the conjugal unit as the reproductive and economic centre of society', a shift that came with the development of stratification.[8] Did that move make things worse for women as is suggested? Whatever the relation with class and women, it is certainly not the case that either nuclear families or small households first emerged at that time. Moreover the structure of some earlier north Germanic settlements was already stratified.

Despite the arguments of German legal historians, there seems little evidence of an 'extended family' in the sense of large households among the peoples that established themselves inside the former Roman Empire. That fact weakens the attempt to relate the evolution of the position of women in Frankish society to the notion of a transition from the 'extended' to the 'restructured' family between the Merovingian (481–?751) and Carolingian (751–?987) periods.[9] While Carolingian rulers and the Church were more insistent on monogamy than had earlier been the case and in that limited sense stressed the conjugal family, there is no adequate evidence of a shift from larger residential groups, only perhaps of a restriction of the wider ranges of relatives. Indeed writing of the Visigoths, it has been suggested that even these ranges already had little power and that it was 'the monogamous family' that now constituted the basic social unit.[10]

Kindreds

How important were early medieval kindreds? It has been argued that Anglo-Saxon England represented a stage on the passage from kinship to lordship, with the kindred losing importance. Certainly lordship came to play a greater part in social life but blood feuds continued to be waged by kin into the eleventh century, later in some parts. Nor was land tenure by any means purely individualistic since customs existed (later known as 'le retrait lignagère') by which kin could bar its members from alienating land to outsiders. Wider ranges of kin (kindreds) remained important in a variety of contexts but their presence in no sense made conjugal families irrelevant; in this society, as in all others, the two were perfectly compatible. In a well-known study Phillpots offers the generalization that where cohesive kindreds persisted into the later Middle Ages, there the peasant or townsman 'tends to be free', offering a different perspective on the role of extended kinship.[11]

Land Sales

Partly owing to the richness of the Anglo-Saxon evidence, the situation in England has often been taken as the model for the early Middle Ages and for later social development more generally, especially in terms of the market, particularly in land. For example, scholars have considered land sales as a 'liberation from a more traditional and restrictive social environment'.[12] The right to alienate has been seen as starting with the church (who had to accumulate from others) and then working its way downward through the secular hierarchy. As Engels remarked of the written will, 'among the Germans it was the clerics who introduced it in order that there might be nothing to stop the pious German from leaving his legacy to the Church'.[13] This development is seen as continuing; 'capitalism did, after all, flower in England first and capitalism is the triumph of the market and of men with entrepreneurial, commercial attitudes to transactions'. Whatever was the case with this fanciful picture, the existence of land sales resulted in a land market, thought to lead to free exchange.

This 'naïve teleology' of capitalist development has been countered by pointing out that whatever the case in England, 'Italians constantly bought and sold land, right from earliest medieval documents'. 'Little restriction on land sales seems to have existed in either Roman or Germanic law in Italy'.[14] Indeed land sales were normal parts of social life not only from the Roman empire but well before in Mesopotamia. Nor were these land transactions confined to men; in Carolingian France in the eighth century, well over 10 per cent involved women.[15] But sales were nevertheless often monitored by kin, at least with regard to inherited (family) land, so there was no absolute opposition between individual and collective rights. Individualism had no obvious beginning, nor collectivism an end. It certainly seems doubtful if individualism (in the form of the sales of land or anything else) can be said to characterize the Anglo-Saxon in any exclusive way (nor yet the Christians, *pace* Dumont).

Collapse of Towns

Other changes did follow the German invasions. After 400 towns in Italy, such as Brescia, collapsed and did not revive for several centuries. But some urban institutions survived, in Italy more than elsewhere. An analysis of land disputes in Lombard–Carolingian Italy from 700 to 900 shows that while cases often concluded with deeds or oath-taking, written evidence became increasingly important. Notaries seem to have persisted and their signatures were required to validate charters. Changes in the rules of evidence meant that written proof took over from purely oral procedures. Many people were familiar with documents and 'documents are almost always about land'.[16]

Feudalism

Subsequently the same authority sees post-Roman Europe as not immediately switching to a feudal regime but only after adopting a 'peasant mode' which was not unstratified but had Big Men giving out as much as they received and therefore not accumulating the surplus with which they could enter into the trade for 'luxury' goods. Until Offa, England was one such society which is compared to Iceland and perhaps to Brittany. In France too elites existed, as witness the account of Gregory of Tours. They ruled by force rather than by earlier gift-giving. However, with the peasant mode the inhabitants were better off than under a feudal regime as they paid no rent to landlords nor tax to the state. On the other hand there were fewer goods they could produce and consume. This regime is seen, in Marxist terms, as a pre-class system, but in fact it is described as existing side by side with 'feudal' regimes which were certainly stratified. Moreover even peasant regimes are usually conceived as typically divided by class, with much of the land being owned by landlords.[17]

That ownership of land clearly influenced family life in fundamental ways since the domestic economy was based on some access to it. In dealing with the family under feudalism, another author stresses the role of the seigneurial system in commanding the labour power of peasants and in encouraging primogeniture.[18] That mode of inheritance (or even other forms of unigeniture which specified one main heir) was especially to be found under the tightly organized open-field agriculture of the manorial system where plots were distributed centrally for one man or family to work. But primogeniture is never absolute; it is always qualified by equity among kin, a kind of distributional ethic among those raised together, which requires some allocation to other siblings. Moreover it is found in systems other than feudal ones, especially where land is a scarce resource. Indeed the notion of a single main heir may well be initiated from below rather than above, as in the rural France of today where the code demands equal division but the practice is very different, for it is recognized that the farm is sufficient to maintain only one family. Nor is primogeniture the only system found under seigneurial domination. The diversity revealed in an authoritative study of inheritance in sixteenth-century France would be incomprehensible from a more determinative point of view and the same could be said for the distribution of gavelkind (equal division), Borough French (primo-geniture) and Borough English (ultimogeniture) in England.[19] But the labour force was heavily controlled in other ways, in paying dues at marriage as well as for various utilities (milling, or even baking bread), in limiting access to village farmland, in imposing services of other kinds (including local courts) and in the kind of generalised demands of obsequience that were mythologized in the notion of 'les droits de seigneur'.

Christianity

In family law, it is claimed, 'Christianity began to exercise an influence only in the mid-eighth century'.[20] This statement refers to the Frankish regions, which were influenced by Roman, Germanic and Christian norms but which still adhered to 'pagan' family practices and in particular to polygyny, concubinage and divorce. These continued to be available until Pepin had dethroned the last Merovingian king in 751; to legitimize his own rule he then 'presented himself as a minister of God responsible for restructuring society according to Christian ideals'.

In effecting those changes in marriage among the Franks, Pepin the Younger found a valuable ally in the English missionary Boniface in the middle of the eighth century. Like Augustine earlier in England, Boniface sought advice from the Pope about what he should do, especially about adultery and incest. The broad prohibitions of the church against marriage within the seventh degree of consanguinity, affinity and spiritual kinship, which defined incest, were then introduced into the Frankish councils. Even to have intercourse with any of these relations was prohibited, leading to a prohibition on any marriage and the confiscation of property (which was added by Charlemagne). As a further measure of control the national synod of Verneuil declared that everybody must marry in public.[21]

The imposition of the church's rules on Germanic society was not immediate or uncontested. At the beginning of the sixth century, royalty was able to disregard incest laws with impunity but by the end of the century the firm stand of the church had its effect; close kinship marriages were dissolved.[22] Of course there was still in-marriage at the class and local levels. Just as the Merovingian elite tended to marry among themselves (though not close kin), so peasants tried to marry daughters within the village.[23] By the end of the sixth century, the church had managed to enforce its incest legislation, prohibiting for example the marriage of one man to two sisters. That was also the case with polygyny which was forbidden by the Visigothic code although, like Roman concubinage, the practice continued among Frankish royalty.

Divorce too was not uncommon until the latter half of the eighth century when 'the Carolingians introduced into both canon and secular law the principle that marriages were binding for life'.[24] It was surely less a question of the Carolingians introducing these practices as of enforcing them more strictly. Divorce by mutual consent seems to have remained popular. However Charlemagne insisted on making divorce more difficult, even excluding adultery as grounds. That decision was reinforced in 829 by four reforming councils forbidding repudiation. A priestly blessing on marriage was advocated by Jonas of Orleans as a safeguard for children's rights of inheritance.

The imposition of these rules in itself revealed much about earlier practices, especially in the resistance put up to the church's hegemony. But in the Carolingian case it also led to a struggle between lay and ecclesiastical models of marriage. By the end of that period the latter was victorious and marriage was enshrined in secular and ecclesiastical legislation as a union binding for life. In the mid-twelfth century the notion of consummation was introduced into the definition of a valid marriage and at the same time women were freed from the necessity of seeking parental consent.[25] Nevertheless traces of earlier customs remained; desertions, abductions, and 'endogamous' unions still persisted.[26]

In establishing its own rules, the church eventually changed the position of women. In Merovingian times, women were the great benefactors of the church in Gaul, as they were at most other periods. By distributing alms, building oratories, extending hospitality and entrusting the education of their children to churchmen, women gained spiritual credit and practical assistance. Elite Merovingian women made important contributions to social life, by 'converting their husbands and children, endowing churches, founding monasteries and dispensing charity'. *Sine manu* marriages disappeared in the Visigothic and Burgundian codes, but while the husband might represent the wife, he could not alienate her property without her consent.[27]

I would see this trend not as a feature of Merovingian and Carolingian society but as embedded in the establishment of the church as a 'great organization'. It is hardly new but grows out of

the situation of women in other major Eurasian societies, where
they were entitled to a portion of the property of their parents.
For the emphasis on the indissolubility of marriage did not change
the established economic position of women in relation to property. On his daughter's marriage, the father gave her property,
including land, as agreed in the negotiations with the prospective
husband. 'This was the dowry, which could alternatively be called
wedd, "pledge" (the origin of the word "wedding"), *wituma*,
dowry; *gifu*, present; or *foederen feoh*, "paternal fee". The husband
himself provided her with the *morgangyfu*, a substantial present of
land or goods, the morning after the marriage had been consum-
mated'. Right from the outset of a marriage the husband had to
declare before the bride's kinsmen 'what he grants her in return for
the acceptance of his suit and what he grants her if she should live
longer than he'.[28] The dowry would be added to the husband's
property during the marriage but if she was a widow without children it was returned to her family at her death. While she lived, she
would enjoy a substantial dower. As a widow with children this
property was largely at her disposition and she might dispose of it
to the church, sometimes to the dismay of her offspring. That
happened in the case of a woman Aescwyn who bequested an estate
at Snodland in Kent to the Bishop of Rochester. 'Her son Aelfric
begrudged this pious act and paid a priest to steal the title deeds
from the bishop.'[29] That conflict between heir and beneficiary
existed throughout the history of the European family.

The prohibition on divorce reduced the dispersal of a man's
property among a number of spouses, with the result, it is
suggested, that fewer women were engaged in transactions in land
after the Carolingian period, though it is not easy to see why.[30] The
bridal gifts were no longer needed as a protection against divorce
as in the eastern Mediterranean but served as a widow's dower, a
protection *after* dissolution. Since women had equal rights of inheritance under Roman law, they appeared as dowagers or widows
in roughly 50 per cent of the charters.[31]

Some of the features that have been attributed to the
Merovingians and Carolingians should be seen as more widely
based in the establishment of Christianity. Others are found more
generally still in the major Eurasian societies. It is argued that the
introduction of monogamy changed the structure of the family
and the transmission of property, at least at the highest level of
society. 'The conjugal family, consisting of husband, wife and children, emerged as the dominant economic unit', excluding

concubines and illegitimate children. 'Elementary families' of various kinds are normally the dominant economic unit in pre-industrial societies, while monogamy (which was present in India and represented a general trend in Eurasia) might also be said to encourage rather than limit concubinage and illegitimacy.[32] In any case we have to be careful not to read too much into what happened at this particular time which may have modified but certainly did not create the conjugal family. Nor did it create conjugal love, which some have attributed to modern Europe but which is correctly perceived as present in narrative sources, donations and wills of Merovingian times. Husband and wife were often buried together.[33] Love and affection between mothers and children is equally clear. But by no means for the first time, as we see from classical and Near Eastern monuments and texts.

With marriage being indissoluble there was increasing pressure on parents to see that their children married properly in the first place so that, it is claimed, there was less hypergamy.[34] But hypergamy (marriage up for the woman, down for the man) is not an improper marriage in a stratified society. Like hypogamy (marriage up for the man, down for the woman) it provides an avenue of social mobility in an otherwise rigid hierarchy; wealth or even beauty can be bargained against prestige and status.[35] There is no evidence of any long term change, for it has always existed in Europe. It is also argued that the serious consequences of a marriage choice led to 'trial marriages', in which the status of the women was as temporary concubines, and that there was more competition for marriage partners. But neither trial marriages nor competition for partners is exclusively related to monogamy.

Earlier Practices Condemned

Some indication of earlier Germanic practices in domestic life is given by Christian objections to what they found. These objections we have come across in the account by Bede of the correspondence between Saint Augustine, the first Archbishop of Canterbury, and the Pope, Gregory, regarding the legitimacy of close marriages in Christian eyes. One other problem that Bede sees is the willingness of parents, especially mothers, to send their children out to wet-nurses (though the rich might bring the nurse into the house). That practice is connected with the fear of changelings, that one's child has been swapped for someone else's, the theme of many a folk tale as long as the practice continued; and it did so, despite the objections of the church, throughout Europe until the twentieth century. It also merged with the general acceptance of fostering, whereby children, often at tender ages, were sent to be looked after by others, sometimes kinsfolk, often not. Later on this propensity of European societies is linked with the giving up of children by single mothers (usually under economic necessity and considerable pressures from family and the authorities) and with the education of children of the upper classes by outside agents (later on in boarding schools). Fostering is a less formal type of adoption (then forbidden) which does not involve a shift of kinship status ('fictional kinship') nor inheritance, but meets some of the other needs for care and upbringing.

The same general themes concerning unchaste (incestuous) marriages that are found in Bede are raised in the section of Saxo Grammaticus' *History of the Danes* which recounts the story Shakespeare later adapted for *Hamlet*. Fengi kills his brother Orvendil and marries his widow Gerutha – 'adding incest to fratricide' comments the author (Bk III, ch. 77). Such marriages were described in the Anglo-Saxon Chronicle as 'heathen custom', meaning that close marriages to the widows of kinsmen (the levirate) had been allowed by non-Christians; Eadbald even married his father's widow.[36] It was a marriage repeated (but condemned by the church) by Aethelbald some 250 years later. Incest was said by the Carolingians to persist in Brittany, which broke from the Frankish church in 846. Even before this, the Bretons were seen as sleeping with their sisters and raping their sisters-in-law.[37]

Part of what may have endured from pre-Christian Europe (especially from Germanic society) were popular forms of marriage such as handfasting, which dispensed with elaborate ritual and ceremony and was perhaps more likely to avoid the panoply of ecclesiastical restrictions. Equally, forms of divorce were developed by the populace, such as the later 'sale of wives'.[38] But that practice probably represents a reaction to those restrictions rather than the continuation of an earlier one. The popular imagination invented ways of getting round the restrictions placed upon their behaviour, restrictions limiting the strategies of heirship that would have benefited the family rather than the church.

One institution that has been claimed to have a longer genealogy in the German lands was known as the kiltgang or bundling.[39] By this practice, young men in the 'lower' strata came to visit their betrotheds and spent part of the night with them in a sexual embrace that fell short, in principle, of full penetration. In fact, it obviously did not always do so since the proportion of pre-marital pregnancies has often been relatively high. However it is probable that the kiltgang too was a later invention since it would hardly be required unless late marriage for men and women prevailed.[40]

Marriages were contracted at an earlier age than in later Europe. Indeed their whole lives were in effect lived out earlier, partly due to early mortality, partly to the fact that in the ninth century women of fourteen were counted as adults before the law. Their formal education began around seven when the boys might be sent to a great lord or to a monastery to be properly brought up. Women seemed to have lived shorter lives than men, having an expectation of 36 years of life in Charlemagne's family. That situation was not general for in the Saxon nobility it was the reverse, although higher mortality occurred among peasant women in the ninth century.[41]

In conclusion, neither the classical nor the Germanic traditions appear to have had an overwhelming effect on the later European family. There were some elements, such as the dowry, that were common to a wider range of Eurasian cultures, others such as love, conjugal or parental, and the elementary family common to a yet wider range of human societies. In other respects much had been transformed by the advent of the Christian Church and its far-reaching but not unresisted attempts to establish new rules for the conduct of domestic life which came to dominate the family in the German lands.

5

European Patterns and Medieval Regimes

Medieval Europe was a largely rural continent, with towns gradually growing up again following the collapse of much urban life after the fall of the Roman Empire. Some trade of course continued but it only began to play a large-scale role again with the rise of Italian commerce in the twelfth century. Well before that happened a strongly class-based society developed in Europe, with patterns of marriage and family differentiated according to one's position in the hierarchy. The elite acted in very different ways from the peasantry.[1] In some respects they were more controlled. Marrying earlier, they were pressured to do so with members of their own group for dynastic reasons. The peasantry usually married other peasants of similar standing but were less constrained in their choice, though interest in access to property was not confined to the elite. And among the peasantry there was a good deal of variability in the way that property was handed down; in England there was gavelkind, Borough French and Borough English; in France, customs varied between what have been called optative and preciput.[2] So too in the Low Countries.

Each of these systems was related to different patterns of household composition which meant these latter could be quite variable.[3] Borough English for example meant that the younger son (the astrier, the one remaining by the hearth) would take over the farm and stay behind with the surviving parents. Other sons had to try and find brides endowed with land, open up new lands as 'assarts' or else look for employment in the towns, in craft occupations elsewhere or as hired hands, possibly remaining on the farm as bachelors. This situation should lead us to modify the view of the family under feudalism which suggests that primogeniture was dominant; the possibilities were broader than that.[4]

Households

Households were mainly based on the nuclear family; it was rare to find three-generation households, although in much of Europe the senior generation would hand over the farm early and retire to the West Room in Ireland, to the old people's house (*alterteil*) in Germany, or elsewhere to a neighbouring property. There they would expect some continuing support from their kin although they had a separate hearth and had given up working and managing the farm. Sometimes this retirement involved the writing of a contract, a kind of *hypothèque*, between the generations, stating the quantities of food and clothing to which they were entitled.[5] Siblings too would usually separate as farmers though they might continue to live nearby and would provide an available source for the supply of equipment to borrow and labour to lend, as was the case in Neckarhausen (Würthemburg) in Germany at a much later period.[6] Structurally however there must have been common features with earlier peasant villages, which justifies us using later evidence for rural practice.[7]

'Houses in Neckarhausen frequently contained more than one married pair . . . throughout the eighteenth and nineteenth centuries, they averaged about 1.4 "families".' That figure, which approximates to the size of 1.59 for 'households' in the Free Royal Cities under the Hungarian Crown (1784–7), is described as falling in the joint family range and therefore as non-western.[8] The proposed dividing line is very thin. These German households normally consisted of close relatives who often shared a kitchen, even when they did not always eat together, for after marriage a son might well apply for his own *Meistershaft* to hold the 'purse strings' while continuing to use all his parents' facilities.[9] Reciprocally, even after such a division the father still had a call on the labour of a son; 'although marriage marked a turning point and began a process of redistributing resources, the period of transition was a long one. Independence marked the first stage, but even then there was no sharp generational turnover and it was a very long time before a young couple got their hands on the old people's property'.[10] It is true that parents and children might pay each other for the labour involved, as the introduction of book-keeping had encouraged very precise notions of exchange. But at the same time they 'cooperated in work or in shared living areas, storage and tools. Sometimes they even advanced each other cash or covered each other's debts'. I refer to this later example from a structurally similar community to make clear the difficulty of distinguishing households (or hearths) and dwelling groups (or 'housefuls'); even when fission had occurred on the farm and produced what were for some purposes separate units, the members still cooperated together in many ways, the result being a complex pattern of overlapping relationships between kin. That complexity makes it less profitable as well as less possible to distinguish between nuclear (or elementary) and extended (or complex) households or dwelling groups, in the medieval period or in any other.

Nuclear Families

At the core of the network of kin relationships there was always a conjugal pair who formed the basis of a nuclear family or household. The existence of wider relationships did not exclude an emphasis on narrower ones. While the emphasis varied, the nuclear family was never totally independent or isolated, especially in rural areas. So it is not easy to decide what was 'the basic unit' in any overall sense.

In discussing the analysis of households in the village of Ruyton,[11] it has been argued that 'what is at issue is the nature of the English family system in the sixteenth and seventeenth centuries . . . . Was the relatively independent nuclear family the basic unit of society or not (with all the implications this might have for our understanding of the interrelated demographic and economic history of the period)?' Or did the ties between extended kin form 'the basis of social relations' in the period?

It is the polarization that is problematic and connected with the 'starke theorie' about the significance of the isolated nuclear family: 'the nuclear family predominates, with or without servants'.[12] I have argued that small domestic groups, approximating to a nuclear family, are found in a large number of societies throughout the world. English households were from one point of view quite complex because they often contained servants who might or might not be related (the well-documented Ralph Josselin took his sister in as a 'servant'). There were relatively few three-generational households but there were of course many three generational families, the members of which helped one another, even if they did not live together.[13] Such co-operation took place in a 'few and untypical' cases in Terling[14], but are the records always detailed enough to provide the kind of information collected for Neckarhausen? On general grounds one would expect the kind of mutual help among kin and kith (neighbours) in village communities of this kind, whether in Europe or elsewhere.

The dispersal of kin ties from the rural areas occurs with the movement to towns, the movement to new farming areas and the movement of craftsmen and artisans. That process may have expanded earlier in England than elsewhere but it was certainly not unique, as some exponents of English exceptionalism assert. Such dispersal did not mean that nuclear families were isolated, except in a superficial way. The Josselin daughters retired home for childbirth and his wife went to London to care for a sick daughter.

Stone views the situation somewhat differently, seeing the medieval period as marked by extended ties of kinship. As with the alternative view, this is a classic case of binarism where the 'lineage (extended) family' is opposed to the nuclear and each are allocated highly general characteristics, such as collective interests versus individual ones. That opposition seems altogether too crude; in the earlier period, individual interests were certainly of great importance, as was the role of the state (collective) in later times.

The central role of the nuclear family in all European countries is emphasized by the kinship terminology but that is especially clear in England because of the interface of the Norman-French and Anglo-Saxon languages after the conquest of 1066. In Anglo-Saxon separate but related terms existed for father (*faeder*) and father's brother (*faedera*) as for mother and mother's sister. Equally in an individual's own generation, the terms for cousins were distinguished from those for brothers and sisters. After 1066 the situation was further highlighted by the fact that the terms for kin outside the nuclear family were abandoned in favour of the Norman-French, while the Germanic roots were retained for the closest kin, mother, father, son, daughter. The nuclear family was isolated linguistically, as happened later in other Germanic areas where French terms were adopted.

Wider Kin Ties

But that group was not isolated in other ways. Kin within a bilateral range (the kindred) were recognized for various social purposes and as we have seen played an important part in people's lives, especially when they were living nearby. In some areas of Europe named patrilineal groups continued to be found; in the Highlands of Scotland as in the mountains of the Balkans, areas where state control was minimal and the existence of wider kin ties important for defensive and offensive purposes (though in Anglo-Saxon England these tasks were organized on a bilateral, kindred, basis). Nor were peripheral regions the only ones where agnatic tendencies were found. There was some agnatic bias in Germanic kin groups, that is, even in a basically bilateral system; and the same was often true when surnames were introduced, Johnson was the son of John. But not everywhere. In the Iberian peninsula systems included or even preferred the mother's name, a fact that like the use of a special term for the mother's brother (*eam* or *emm* in lowland Scots) has also been wrongly taken as a survival of earlier matrilineal clans. Surnames were a later development. The study of medieval kinship in Europe is complicated by the fact that the bulk of the people had no surnames or only topographic ones; there was no *gens*, not even patronymics, so that relationships become difficult to follow (as they no doubt were for the actors).

Wider kinship groups, indeed types of lineage, contined to exist in parts of southern Europe, especially among the elite. Apart from the Balkans and the Scottish Highlands, we find distinct patrilineal groups in some rural areas like Corfu but more spectacularly among the elite in certain cities in Italy where they seem to have been reinvented as mechanisms of support in the politically fluid situation of city-states.[15] Florence is the best analysed case. Groups of agnates, which might be associated with a tower or form a *consorteria*, acted defensively and offensively. Their collective responsibility was recognized by the communal government in the fourteenth century; the vendetta was allowed, even for the common folk, but increasingly regulated by law. For the elites (the magnates), the bounds of agnatic responsibility were considerably wider than for others, leaving them with the duty of punishing a wrong-doer both within and outside the lineage. However the overall aim of the commune was to stifle private violence and to reserve to itself the right of ultimate control; it also undertook the increasing supervision of other kinship matters, permitting migrants to be treated as Florentine born and illegitimate children to become heirs.[16] In general kin networks seem to have shrunk by the end of the Middle Ages. Central governments now looked after law and order, so that wider kin groups like armed factions tended to become things of the past.

Mentalities and Childhood

For historians of the family who adopt the notion of 'mentalité', the medieval period forms the dramatic backdrop, the sharp contrast, to the modern family. Ariès, for example, sees the notion of childhood as emerging in sixteenth-century Europe at a time when the life of children is said to have become more highly valued.[17] It was when infant mortality began to drop, he suggests, that parents could afford to lavish love on their children without the ever-present danger of them being snatched from them. In fact, infant mortality continued to be high until the end of the nineteenth century. And in any case there is little evidence that the level of grief (or of love) is related to the number of children a parent has had, although the disappointment may be greater if the holding is smaller. Medievalists have queried this view of the Middle Ages, anthropologists have done the same for other cultures.[18] There seems to have been an important culture of childhood in China but it is clearly superficial to think that the range of toys, which has been taken as an indicator, correlates with the level of affection.

Nevertheless the notion of Ariès about a shift of 'mentalities' in the modern period has been taken up by Stone and in a different way by those others who see the so-called affective family as characteristic of that as distinct from the medieval period.[19] I do not think it is possible to sustain this thesis about a quantum jump in Europe.[20] Certainly medieval scholars have strongly criticised the conclusions of Stone about earlier European domestic life and those criticisms would be upheld by anthropological research.[21] Changes of course there were but to conceive of these in terms of a shift from the Open Lineage Family (of 1450–1630) to the Restricted Patriarchal Nuclear Family (of 1550–1700), as Stone does, is to over-formalize and over-generalize what happened in a misleading way. The bulk of the population of western Europe did not have lineages at any point and they lived largely in nuclear family households. The notion of dramatic psycho-sociological changes, so often embodied in the work of the mentalité approach, does injustice to the course of events, leading to a neglect of continuing features (such as small, core 'families') and over-emphasizing the uniqueness of each period, especially in relation to the modern family, here characterized by 'affective individualism'. The whole emphasis placed by these writers on the 'affective' nuclear family of modern times seems to overlook subsequent developments in domestic lives and to mis-understand earlier ones. Such psychological variables are not clearly enough identified to contribute greatly to sociological or historical analysis.

The Demographic Approach

An alternative, mainly demographic, approach to the modern family stresses the continuities with the medieval period, especially in England where the small isolated 'affective' family is thought to have been present much earlier and to have paved the way for later developments in society. A related question about the possible continuities and differences between medieval and modern societies has to do with the emergence of the so-called European marriage pattern and the associated features. It had been a common assumption of historians that pre-industrial households were characterized by extended or expanded 'families' which meant that the mean size (or structure) was much larger than in recent times. The work of Laslett and his associates in the Cambridge Group, examining a series of English parish records dating from the sixteenth century, showed that as long as those records existed, households have been relatively small and that there was no evidence for the previous assumption. These house-holds were based on late marriage with some 50 per cent of children going out at adolescence to work on neighbouring farms as living-in servants, working either on the land or in the house. When they wanted to marry they had to leave their employers and set up house on their own. Marriage was delayed, experience gained, a peculium accumulated and independence won. In this account late marriage for men is reckoned to be over 26 years, for women over 23.[22]

European Marriage Pattern

For others these particular features are characteristic of what Hajnal has called the European marriage pattern, in fact a north-western pattern, which is contrasted with most of the rest of the world and which is seen as associated with smaller households and as contributing to that region's development of capitalism. Men and women were accustomed to going out to work before marriage (and hence before the interventions of childbirth) and saving to set up their own households (in fact endowing themselves). Later marriages also led to certain features that were associated with modernization, fewer parents and grandparents, fewer complex households, more options in the choice of partner and more ex-perienced parenting and child care.

Household Formation

Subsequently Hajnal shifted his attention from mean size of house-hold (MSH), which was found not to differ so greatly as between Europe and the rest, to household formation. He contrasted north-western Europe with Tuscany, which is compared to present-day Maharashtra (India), the former having a simple system of house-hold formation, the latter a 'joint system'.[23] The simple system is marked by late marriage and in-living servants, so is less 'simple' than it appears; the joint household, because of earlier marriage, contains two married couples (hence more 'children') and fewer in-living servants. Was that also the situation in medieval times? Was there continuity rather than difference? The evidence is thin, but less so for some supposedly associated features. There is early evidence for the presence of large numbers of life-cycle servants, mainly found in the north of Europe, fewer in the South;[24] secondly, for retirement contracts which in recent times were more frequent in Finland, Central Europe and Southern France, less so in England; thirdly, for the greater public provision for the poor that enabled people better to control their fertility since they did not have to plan for children to support them in later life. Traces of these three features were to be found in England four centuries prior to 1600, which is taken as evidence for the earlier presence of the European marriage pattern in the medieval period and specifically in England, and which is suggested as its original home.[25] But none of these features, especially the third which was hardly general in European societies, is exclusively linked to England nor yet to Europe; charitable provision was made in the other major civilizations. Nor are high rates of celibacy only to be found there; these are logically consistent with late marriage and formed part of Hajnal's original European marriage pattern. Certainly some of these features were well developed in Europe, some at least in late medieval times, but this was never an exclusive association, nor is it apparent how they were necessarily linked to the development of capitalism. The mercantile variety was found in other parts of the world with different constellations of kinship variables, so that the specific contribution of any one of these sets to subsequent developments is far from clear; alternative scenarios could and have led to similar results. Hence except in an ethnographic sense, the question of the age and location of these features is less important for the socio-cultural history of capitalism than many western scholars have thought.

Late Marriage and In-living Servants

What does seem to be a significant difference between Europe and most other parts of the world is the lateness of marriage and the number of in-living servants. In a Danish sample for 1645 over 50 per cent of those who survived past adolescence had been in service, with servants constituting between 6 and 15 per cent of the total population at any one time. That figure is certainly related to late marriage (and to marriage permanently postponed), contrasting with many Asian societies where marriage, especially for women, was early (the classic case is Hindu India), where there are few living-in servants (but plenty of service) and where parents are younger, the generations shorter and residential fission occurs later in the domestic cycle. In Europe that contrast may well have preceded the Renaissance but it seems questionable that this constellation predicted modernity in the ways suggested.[26]

The remarkable work of the Cambridge Group that stressed these features is based upon household listings and parish records. Some have pointed to problems of analysing kinship relations on the basis of such documents.[27] Households and families have tended to be considered as 'natural units'. Despite the general claim that servants were not kin of their employer, in Ryton (in Tyne and Wear) 'perhaps a third' of all those who left home (and not all did so) went to stay with kin.[28] A similar question arises with the transfer of land. The author suggests in her analysis of the same village, 'Where change has been considered, it has been in terms of broad historical change – industrialization or 'modernization' – with household structure seen as either cause or effect.'[29] Modernisation theory requires the abandonment of wider kinship ties. But how far did land transactions occur between kin? Did such internal transactions predominate?[30] It has been shown that even for the late seventeenth century many land sales were contracted with kin (though for more money than with outsiders!). Most transactions, including sales, were with equals, but some were made with the church, part as gifts, part as sales.

Christian Norms

The Christian norms about marriage, sexuality and divorce continued to be of major significance in medieval Europe.[31] But we have to distinguish between the general values promoted by the church and the actual regulations administered and sanctioned by ecclesiastical and secular law. Regarding the general values, neither the view of Christian marriage as existing primarily for procreation and child rearing, nor those regarding contraception, abortion, homosexual relations and heterosexual acts for pleasure, were as susceptible to regulation as divorce. There was another life going on in the world in which Christian restraints played little part and this life had more than a court existence; on quite another level, it was freely expressed in Boccaccio's *Decameron*, an urban collection of tales which furnished 'pleasurable and subversive depictions of a society in thrall to fornication and adultery'.[32]

Resistance

Of course, the church never had it all its own way, although its influence was extensive. It moved towards the equal treatment of men and women in domestic matters and against the role of kin groups like the Montagues and the Capulets; indeed Romeo and Juliet emphasizes the liberating role played by the church in the question of choice of partner. Conflicts clearly developed between the norms and jurisdiction of church and state (and simply of general practice). The *jus occidendi* (law of homicide) in *jus commune* (common law) was an unequal affair, applying to women's adultery but not to men's, as was its extension to other killings for the sake of honour. It was used in Italy, Spain and Germany at least until the eighteenth century. But it ran quite against the law of the church which insisted that husband and wife must be judged by the same standards. Later Enlightenment critics took up the objections to practices based on seeing society as a union of families rather than as a union of individuals. However, the notion of an honourable killing, allowed to men and not women, continued in Italian law until 1981, linking female sexuality to largely male family honour. The problem was intrinsic to the treatment of adultery as a whole throughout Europe.

Conflicts of another kind arose within secular law that also affected the family. Local laws differed but a knowledge of supralocal values and standards of conduct coming from Christian doctrines and Roman and canon law is necessary to understand them. Roman law also continued to act as a point of reference, especially after the growth of the great law schools in Northern Italy and in contexts that were not specifically considered by the councils of the church. In the twelfth century a struggle took place between the Romanists around Gratian and the School of Bologna who wanted marriage to be founded on consummation (as in Roman law) and the canonists (especially Peter Lombard and the French School) who wanted it to be founded on mutual consent. It was the latter who carried the day as far as the church was concerned. But while secular law and norms filled in the interstices, the sway of the church still held for a wide range of regulations in family life, breaches of which were dealt with by ecclesiastical courts. A modification of these came only with the Renaissance, the Reformation and the ensuing Enlightenment, and to those developments we now turn.

6

Women, Children and Fathers in the Reformation and Counter-Reformation

Changes in the European family after the Renaissance are often discussed in terms of the economic developments that were taking place at that time, the development of the market, in particular the external markets, the changes in agriculture and in urban life, in the commercial and manufacturing base that accompanied this development, not to speak of more local shifts on a country to country basis. The growth of towns obviously created a different relation between family, household and livelihood than existed in rural areas. These relationships are difficult to establish, as with demographic changes, partly because of the relative dearth of both quantitative and qualitative material before the sixteenth century, although we have useful studies of Florentine and Belgian towns in the fifteenth and fourteenth centuries, as well as of English villages in the thirteenth.[1] The result has been much disagreement about the European family in the early modern period, regarding the way it has either assisted or been transformed by the other major changes that were taking place.

I suggest that the changes in 'mentality' or in structure were less radical than has often been suggested; for far-reaching shifts in the domestic order related to the economy we have to wait until the effects are felt of the expansion first of proto-industrialization and then of industrialization. However changes did take place and many of the important among these were related to two processes: to altered religious practices and beliefs brought about by the Reformation and Counter-Reformation; and to the process of secularization given a strong boost by the Renaissance of learning and developments in knowledge systems, especially during the Enlightenment. Both had the effect of weakening earlier norms embodied in Christian teaching and activity, which were linked not only to a theological system but as we have seen to ways of supporting the church as a 'great organization' rivalling in some respects the power of the state. With the deliberate disbanding of certain elements of that organization by the Protestants, in particular the monastic arm, the church no longer needed or received all the support it had formerly had, so under the new dispensation people generally benefited from the circulation of that part of the church's wealth as well as being relieved of the need to contribute in the way they had before.

Changing Rules of Permitted Marriages

So, if religion and the property demands of the church had been so important features in the regulation of family life in Europe, it was inevitable that when these changed, so too would the norms of family life. Nowhere is this clearer in Protestant England in the late sixteenth century where it was not only a question of individual Protestants, or a Protestant sect, but of a state-supported Anglican Church. The new uncertainty emerges from the correspondence of Archbishop Parker which suggests that the inhabitants did not know what to do about marriage prohibitions when the Catholic rules were cast aside. There were no longer established norms to which they should conform; uncertainty reigned regarding which marriages were permitted. It is arguable that we should see certain of the themes in Shakespeare and more generally in Elizabethan drama as reflecting this very doubt, this rethinking of the bases of domestic life, where kings might sleep with the wives of their dead brothers (forbidden by the Catholic church but encouraged under Judaic law, which Henry accepted and then rejected) and thus devastate the lives of their nephews and nieces.[2]

That state of affairs is apparent in the account of a cultural critic. 'The attempted annulment of Henry VIII's marriage to Catherine of Aragon generated an enormous literature which profoundly affected Reformation thinking on the relationship between natural, divine and civil law. The perplexity of the arguments pertaining to the Henrician case demonstrated a persistent uncertainty belying centuries of apparently authoritative comment and exegesis'.[3] In other words, challenge the ecclesiastical prescription and uncertainty reigns. Despite the appeals to natural law, no consensus emerged. Luther recognized only the rules of Leviticus, which being divine allowed of no dispensation. Calvin saw Leviticus as the divine expression of natural law and argued for the 'customary' prohibition on the marriage of first cousins and both allowed and disallowed the levirate. Family life was confused 'as normative ideals of natural law (sic) gave way under the combined onslaughts of Calvinism, scepticism, rationalism and empirical science'.[4] The very notion of what was *incasta* (incestuous) was subject to an uncertainty which infuses so much of Elizabethan drama.

The situation of uncertainty in England did not last long. The Anglican church established its own rules and courts, modifying earlier regulations; elsewhere too Protestants adopted variations of the prohibited degrees and sought, at an ideological level, to put more stress on family responsibility, though it is not always easy to see how this translated into practice.

The prohibitions on marriage therefore changed radically in certain parts of Europe with the abandonment by Protestants of many of the rules and of the concurrent system of indulgences and dispensations. But change also gradually took place within the Catholic community. That happened in Corsica where the domestic group was characterized by predominantly nuclear households, although some *frèreches* did exist; but neighbouring households containing close relatives collaborated in daily life, especially in economic activities. The core range of kin to the fourth degree, in which marriage was prohibited by the church, was the one which supported each other in the vendetta, particularly important as a jural procedure in hill areas outside the control of the central government.

Despite the fact that within this range marriage was prohibited by the church, change happened gradually over time. From the eighteenth century that institution increasingly gave dispensations for such unions. Indeed in the region of Niola between 1875 and 1920 the percentage of kin marriages rose to 41.5 per cent while between 1926 and 1950 Corsica had a rate of 8.2 per cent such marriages, more than any other French department.[5]

Women

The Reformation did affect the position of women, where the changes came to affect Catholics as well. As we have seen, Christianity was associated in various ways with promoting the position of women (and children), and not only with regard to the family or for the transmission of property. Female saints numbered about a quarter of the total. In the first phase these women were largely drawn from the rich who founded or ran ecclesiastical institutions; they were the beneficiaries of wealth who themselves benefited spiritually and by renown from their charity. But from the thirteenth century their number included Holy Maids of more lowly origin who were often marked out by visions and similar experiences. These women were later discouraged by the Counter-Reformation and left aside altogether by the Protestants who downplayed the role even of more established saints and insisted on the word of God rather than of intermediaries, let alone on the image or other distractions of the senses. Nuns and convents disappeared in the process. Both movements of reform stressed chastity and obedience, seeing ignorance as a main enemy and promoting the benefits of schooling for women as well as for men.

Nuns had long been interested in the education of girls which led to the problems with seclusion. Some had already struggled against their enclosure in monasteries, while others such as Arcangela Tarabotti (1604–52) had taken up a feminist stance, as did Mary Ward (1585–1645) over education in the Low Countries and England. The Ursulines initially performed good works outside the cloister and by the later seventeenth century in France other women (mainly widows) assisted in the work, especially of the Sisters of Charity, in reclaiming prostitutes, helping the poor and sick, and carrying out charitable and educational activities of a semi-professional kind.

Partly as a result of these efforts, by 1800 just over a third of women in France (although twice as many men) could write their own names. In the north the average was higher, in the south lower. As for charity, by the time of the Revolution, one in every 120 Frenchwomen was committed to a life of good works demanding celibacy and chastity, a situation that did not exist in Protestant countries. Indeed Florence Nightingale declared that if Britain had had the Sisters of Charity, there would have been no need for her.[6] For in Protestant countries there was not the same organized role for widows as in Catholic ones; they were thrown more on their own resources, on the help of their families, and on the support of the community. While the Catholic church provided an accepted, non-domestic role for women, there was a sense in which some Protestant women were 'forced to be free'; the individualist, Anne Locke, left her husband behind when she followed the Marian exiles to Geneva and in doing so helped to redefine the role of women in England, following her own spiritual path to salvation. With the coming of the Civil War that movement expanded rapidly among the separatist religious sects – a movement encouraged by the printing press. In Holland, women even held a few minor offices in the Calvinist church. The position of women in bourgeois Flanders in the sixteenth century was certainly different from that in other parts of Europe. At the end of that century a Spanish historian noted that 'They read, wrote, compared passages of scripture and disputed the faith like highly learned doctors'.[7] In the England of the following century women even founded some break-away congregations, while in the 1640s the Leveller wives came out very strongly in support of their imprisoned husbands, bringing upon themselves the name of fishwives (renowned for shouting their wares) but refusing to keep quiet. Women also played a notable part in other sects, in the early Quaker movement as well as in Methodism.

Societies of this period have often been described as 'patriachal' and certainly some aspects of domestic life were often dominated by males when they were present. But the part played by women, somewhat differently in Protestant than in Catholic communities, should not be underrated. In the discussion of kinship in the propertyless classes of western Europe in the nineteenth century that was based on autobiographies, the centrality of the mother is noted, 'nearly half the fathers being remembered as unable or unwilling to fulfil their basic parental responsibilities'.[8] Even when the father was around, the mother was often the most important figure; when he died, she it was who had effective custody, and she it was who had to work her fingers to the bone to provide for herself and the children. Factory production had helped to marginalize the father, but unless we appreciate the role of women, especially in relationship to the care and support of children, it is difficult to understand the present situation in Europe. That cannot be done by way of gross contrasts between the traditional and the modern. One central aspect of women's position in European society has always related to the dowry which she received at marriage and, while it was often controlled by the husband as part of the conjugal fund, remained in the end her property. That system I consider in greater depth in the following chapter.

The Dissolution of Marriage: Divorce

In other respects the position had not greatly changed. Divorce was prohibited by all Christian communities, although it was possible to annul marriages on certain grounds such as male impotency. Separation was an alternative involving the return of the dowry, but that did not permit remarriage, except to a limited extent among Calvinists; in Scotland, for example, in the second half of the seventeenth century, there occurred less than one divorce a year. In England from the late seventeenth century it became possible for a husband (usually an aristocrat) to bring a civil action against a wife, which has been seen as ushering in the official disintegration of elite marriage.[9] But it was so minor a move that the virtual indissolubility of marriage in England was scarcely affected until the mid-nineteenth century, although in France the situation changed temporarily in 1792 with the Revolution when approximately three times as many women as men took advantage of the possibility of initiating divorce; it served as a new release for women more than for men who had found it easier to abscond. The early modern period also saw a rise in marriage litigation and the increasing role of the lawyer skilled in arguing the case for separation and for the consequent monetary arrangements, including the payment of fees to themselves, as they became increasingly involved in domestic affairs.

In medieval England the ecclesiastical courts had jurisdiction over much of domestic life, especially marriage, although some of their powers were challenged by the state and by the common law. But the main challenge came in the 1530s with the victory of Protestantism and the assumption of headship of the church by Henry VIII. Royal control over many aspects of the church had already been a reality long before 1500. But it was not until the Henrician Reformation that 'the church was finally and decisively subjected to the crown'.[10] It seemed possible at this moment that the ecclesiastical courts would be all but destroyed and that the bulk of their business pass under secular control. Nevertheless they continued to exist, not with the same authority as before but with important spheres of jurisdiction especially in domestic matters.

While they were abolished by the Commonwealth, since Puritans regarded them with grave suspicion, the courts were revived in 1660 and continued to play a role even into the eighteenth century. They still continued to correct fornicators, adulterers and other moral offenders, probably receiving a large measure of popular support.[11]

However most marital disputes that still came before the ecclesiastical courts in France, England and in Europe generally were related not to the breakdown of marriage but to breaches of promise in setting it up, not to its dissolution but to its failed establishment. The majority of the suits concerning the breakdown of relationships in Bologna between 1544 and 1563 were for breach of promise (50 per cent), then came annulment (23.1 per cent), separation (16.7 per cent) and bigamy (10.2 per cent).[12] Once again women initiated the action in 54 per cent of the cases and emerged as the winning party in 87 per cent. Women were seen not only as favoured by the church but as freer to act because of their 'exclusion as heirs', although they had earlier received a portion as dowry.

This clinging to the indissolubility of marriage has been explained above all by 'religious conviction'.[13] The pagan Romans had certainly allowed divorce and remarriage. On the other hand, many other peoples, such as the Zulu of South Africa, do not do so, on what appear to be social or at least customary grounds. Even where divorce is allowed, strong feelings often run against dissolution and in favour of the permanence and uniqueness of marriage, as witnessed for example in the respect paid by the Romans to a woman (*univirae*) who had had only one husband. There was a widespread tendency to deprecate the end of a union even when its ending was permitted, a sentiment that prefigured the possibility of a complete ban. The pressures on continuity may be social and familial as well as religious but Christianity strongly reinforced the trend, adding strong religious sanctions.

One result of the virtual impossibility of divorce and remarriage was a 'high tolerance of marital violence and sexual infidelity'. For men with their greater opportunities for dalliance, their physical strength, their mobility, there was far less reason to object to this state of affairs.[14] And indeed there were sometimes other ways to this end by means of a private set of informal transactions (for example, buying one's freedom) in addition to the ecclesiastically regulated ones. Hence it followed that, when given the chance, women initiated dissolution more frequently than men, despite all the difficulties involved in financial arrangements (the return of the dowry, the subsequent diminution of support), the custody of the children (which could be threatened and lost) and the resulting ignominy of being a lone parent in a society dominated by conjugal couples who were favoured by the law.

The Dissolution of Marriage: Death

However, due to frequent dissolution of marriage not by divorce but by death, the co-resident family was often a complex one, with husbands remarrying at the death of a wife and establishing more complex domestic units that gave rise to step-parenthood and half-siblinghood. Remarriage was somewhat more difficult for widows with young children and particularly for poor women beyond child-bearing age. Throughout the seventeenth century the church 'was becoming more interested in the widow's energies and in the funds she might command'.[15] As the eighteenth-century historian Gibbon stressed, that interest existed at the very beginning of Christianity. The widow who had repossessed her dowry was particularly valued. She was entitled to whatever she had brought into the marriage (the dowry) or, by agreement, the income on this sum. She could claim her clothes, jewellery and whatever her husband had settled on her, a third (or half) of what they communally owned (after marriage) and whatever else he cared to bestow. In the north of the continent, she was considered the natural guardian of the children during their minority and some widows remained in their conjugal homes as heads of households (as many as 10–15 per cent in France). But in the south the husband's family usually had the responsibility for looking after the children and the widow might receive nothing more than her dowry. Indeed his kin might even claim the business he had established and to which she had contributed, leaving the widow 'distressed', unable to continue with their joint work. Elsewhere she could try to run his business independently, without being beholden to her own or to her husband's kin. That possibility was more likely among artisans than in the upper groups, although women like the Wyf of Bath or those appearing in collections such as the Paston letters remind us that there, too, women could attain a degree of independence.[16] But in the lower groups there were a significant number of female heads of household, which together with those living alone amounted to roughly 20 per cent in the artisanal parish of St Apollinare in Rome in the early eighteenth century; female-headed households were more common in the poor parishes, partly because that was where lone women who experienced poverty moved. Such widows had few problems regarding the custody of children nor were there financial interests that made them return to their families of origin; their autonomy was much greater than women from the propertied classes. In almost one-third of the households headed by women, they lived alone; over 8 per cent lived *a compagnia* with another, unrelated, woman, a strategy of survival promoted by the low rates of female wages and the desire for female companionship. There was of course a great difference in the proportion of women working for wages depending on class. In the textile quarter of Santa Maria della Carità in Bologna in 1796 almost the same number of women (73.9 per cent) as men were employed; in the middle class areas it was very much less (28 per cent if we exclude the employment of domestic servants).

The Protestant church always saw marriage as the more desirable end for widows. The large majority of younger ones remarried, though not as frequently as widowers; in seventeenth-century Germany 80 per cent of those married within a year. Marriages lasted about 16 to 20 years and the woman lived slightly longer than the man. But of course she was usually younger than her husband, especially in southern Europe, so there were many more widows than widowers. However in those parts widows were much less likely to remarry.[17] They were not necessarily heads of families. In towns some clustered together to sustain a livelihood and it was more difficult for them to inherit a rural patrimony against the claims of the husband's kin. Indeed their frequency made southern cities into what have been called 'widow-capitals'.[18] In 1525 Seville was described by the Venetian ambassador as a city 'in the hands of women', partly due to the migration of men to the New World. Meanwhile in the seventeenth century Amsterdam had a large number of lone women because of the sailors who were either drowned at sea or simply stayed in the East Indies. Many widows were poor; in Catalan assessments of 1780–1800 they accounted for half of those receiving alms. In their distress many had to make a living in 'an economy of expediency', sometimes pasturing a cow on a neighbour's land, often being reprimanded for so doing, replying with curses and getting stigmatised as a witch.

However, poverty was certainly not the fate of all widows, some of whom were recipients of wealth (their own and their husband's),

were prized as spouses (the 'merry' widow) and often did marry
again, especially if they were young. In France in the first half of
the eighteenth century those aged between 20 and 29 had a 67 per
cent chance as compared with 80 per cent for widowers. In England
the figures were much higher. In all European societies the greater
prominence of widows as compared with widowers was partly due
to differences in marriage age, partly to women's greater longevity
and partly to their control of wealth, or lack of it.

Sex

One difference in the post-Reformation situation lay in the greater
likelihood that in Protestant countries sexual misconduct would be
attacked. In Calvinist Geneva adulterous couples could be expelled.
In Germany municipal brothels were closed down, whereas they
had been actively promoted by Dominicans in the fifteenth century
as a way of protecting respectable women. Brothels do not seem to
have existed to any extent in earlier Britain, Scandinavia or the
Netherlands ('the north'), while in Mediterranean countries the
offical recognition of prostitution may have reflected the higher
differential in the marriage age of men and women, and the presence of celibate clerics. In Renaissance Europe, Rome became the
early capital of prostitution, and with Venice was the centre of
the culture of the courtesan. However that north–south difference
did not last. Nor did the confessional split. Later on Paris and
London rivalled the Italian states for the number of whores. In
eighteenth-century Paris approximately one woman in thirteen
looked to prostitution for a least part of her income; the trade
became increasingly professionalized but nevertheless remained
largely amateur and in the hands of women.

While Protestantism tried, not very successfully, to put an end to
the practice (Luther gave dowries to official prostitutes) and all
fornicators, male and female, were debarred from the Kingdom of
Heaven, the Counter-Reformation also made it less visible in
Catholic lands. By the late seventeenth century the licensed brothel
had generally disappeared and in Italy the Counter-Reformation
tried to convert the penitent prostitute (the Mary Magdalene) into
a potential nun through its many foundations for rescuing 'fallen
women'.[19] There was a general change over time which seems to
have been influenced by the Reform.

Unmarried Mothers: Italy and England

By the seventeenth century the Counter-Reformation had other effects on the family, for example in modifying the traditional responsibility of men for the care of their illegitimate offspring. If married men were held responsible, it was felt, his legitimate family would suffer. Hence such children should be looked after in orphanages. In Protestant countries, on the other hand, men continued to be held personally responsible and relatively few infants were given up.[20] Elsewhere, the search for paternity was gradually abandoned, notably during the French Revolution after initial efforts had been made to erode the distinction between legitimate and illegitimate children. Even in England efforts were made to ban paternity suits, but these were only partially successful.

That situation touches upon another broad difference between Catholic and Protestant countries, namely their treatment of unmarried mothers and foundlings. The abandonment of children in Europe goes back at least to Rome where it constituted a way of adjusting family size to parental resources, a kind of postnatal birth control falling short of outright infanticide. It has been estimated that urban Romans abandoned as many as 20 to 40 per cent of their children in the first three centuries of the Christian era and in the early Middle Ages large numbers continued to be so treated, the parent's poverty being regarded as an adequate justification.[21] The church did not itself favour these practices, yet infanticide remained common as did abandonment (which it did not condemn). In the early Middle Ages abandoned children in Italy were looked after by the local parish where the *matricularii*, the officials in charge of the poor, placed them in families who gave them a variety of statuses, ranging from servant to heir, in this way partially counteracting the ban on adoption. With the twelfth century and the development of hospital foundations such as Les Maisons Dieu, foundlings began to be cared for by these charities. In Italy special establishments such as the Innocenti in Florence were started to take charge of them. In France a few such institutions were established and at the initiative of the monarchy in Portugal too. The movement expanded in the sixteenth and seventeenth centuries after the Counter-Reformation, even reaching Protestant England where it resulted in the foundation of Christ's Hospital, London. Like the move to establish dowry funds for poor women, these establishments were part of an effort to use the public sphere of the state as well as that of the church to handle social problems. Some were municipal, others ecclesiastical.

The presence of these institutions, which spread from Italy to other parts of Europe, meant that the fathers had no final responsibility for their illegitimate children, while the mothers were not permitted to bring up (or in many cases even feed) their own offspring in what were regarded as morally reprehensible circumstances, so they had to hand them over to the homes. As a result many of the children died in early infancy, despite the efforts of their carers.

At the Reformation the Protestants took the line that mothers should bring up their own children and both parents should take individual responsibility for their sins. The Catholics continued to advocate institutional help but the Counter-Reformation tried to tighten up notions of marriage and legitimacy, insisting that lawful child-bearing could take place only within a marriage blessed by the church. While under ecclesiastical law bastards could be legitimized by the subsequent marriage of their parents, English common law decreed that 'once a bastard, always a bastard'. Those who cohabited outside of marriage could be excommunicated. So there was a decrease in illegitimacy in the late sixteenth century. Women however were no longer protected by the earlier customary unions validated merely by the promise to marry.

Illegitimate children had to be baptized as soon as possible to ensure their souls were saved. Even the foetus or the neonate of a mother who died in childbirth had to be extracted by a Caesarian operation in order to be blessed. In Italy illegitimate children continued to be left in foundling hospitals although in nineteenth-century France that applied to under half the total number of such children.[22] The reasons for this difference lay partly in the greater emphasis on honour and shame in the south. Female honour was closely connected with their sexuality, which had to be protected by men. Otherwise both men and women in a family lost honour, leading on the one hand to efforts to cover up the birth and on the other to taking revenge against those responsible for dishonouring the woman, a revenge that was often approved by members of the community who were willing to overlook the condemnations of the national law.

Throughout Europe in the sixteenth century ecclesiastical courts were increasingly unwilling to recognize informal marriages, including the clandestine ones that were numerous in Protestant

England until 1754, thus bastardizing any offspring.[23] In 1556 a law to this effect was made by Henri II in France who also issued an edict laying down the death penalty for unmarried women concealing their pregnancy or the birth of a child that had died before baptism. Similar obligations to declare a pregnancy were established in England, Portugal and most of the Italian states.[24]

Children

Changes also took place in the situation of children. In the mid-sixteenth century in France, and some seventy years later in England, stringent laws were enacted against infanticide (seen principally as a woman's crime, although men too could obviously be involved in the slaughter of the innocents). The two Reformations were both concerned with children dying before baptism, especially as the result of human intervention, by abortion or by infanticide. Infanticide accounted for a significant proportion of all homicide cases and was especially associated with unmarried mothers. To combat this state of affairs The French law of 1556 obliged a mother to declare and register her pregnancy and to reveal the name of the father, partly to ensure where the responsibility for support lay. At certain times failure to fulfil this obligation invoked the death penalty.

A similar law was introduced to England in 1624 but women gradually became treated more leniently, and the law was eventually repealed in 1803. The French law was abolished at the Revolution, at which time, unlike England, there was a steep rise in the number of reported cases of infanticide.

Abandoned children in the south (though for specific reasons there were virtually none in Sardinia) were mainly illegitimate. But in the towns of Milan and Florence families also left legitimate children at these homes as part of their economy of expediency. That continued to be the case and in Milan at the end of the nineteenth century, three-quarters of illegitimate children were abandoned, but over half of the abandoned children were legitimate (a third of all legitimate births).[25] The percentage of legitimate children among those abandoned shows some interesting variation over place and time. It was 28 per cent in Rennes on the eve of the Revolution, and 64 per cent in Milan in 1854. The costs of such non-familial parenting was considerable, whether carried out by charity or from the public purse. In Portugal at this time the maintenance of abandoned children took up to 40–50 per cent of the municipal budget.

There was always a mix of public support and private benefaction, the former mediated by the state, the latter usually by the church. But the weight placed upon one or the other was very different at difficult times. I take post-Reformation England as an example of the balance of provision by the civil administration rather than the ecclesiastical authorities, a secularization that prefigures the present state of affairs in Europe.

The Elizabethan Poor Law had made such dependence quite explicit, since it put the responsibility squarely 'on the parish'. It did so by supporting the mother and trying to get the father to pay. The original Poor Law, established by an Act of Elizabeth, compelled the putative father of a bastard child to maintain it by weekly payments on pain of imprisonment. But that legislation proved ineffective. An Act of Charles II allowed churchwardens and overseers, on the orders of two Justices, to attach the goods and chattels or the rents of the parents to provide for the child. An Act of 1810, replacing a harsher statute of James I, enabled any two Justices to commit 'a lewd woman' who had a chargeable bastard to the House of Correction. This statute was rarely enforced.

By the eighteenth century legislation of George II and George III any justice could issue a warrant for the arrest of the putative father if a single woman became pregnant and charged a man with paternity. It was this law that the Poor Law Commissioners reporting in 1834 saw as giving rise to the grossest inequities. A woman could force a man into marriage under threat of imprisonment. The alternative was to persuade her to have an abortion or for him to abscond; in the latter case the local overseers could pay her a weekly allowance out of the poor rate.

Such support gave rise to similar complaints as we find today. The system was said to incite perjury, to encourage non-marital intercourse, to undermine modesty and self-reliance, and to place a premium on early and improvident marriages. And it was expensive on the citizens since the parish only recovered half of the payments it made. The determination of paternity had previously depended not only upon the woman's claim but upon the man's acceptance or denial. Her claim was more powerful if supported by an oath, especially if that oath were made '*in extremis doloribus partibus*', that is, while she was experiencing the extreme pains of childbirth.[26] Before the sixteenth century, the presumed father rarely denied having had sexual relations.[27] But if he did so after having made a promise to marry, he could not be forced to enter into a union because of the doctrine of mutual consent. The judge could only award damages. Later on the church's attitude to marriage became much stricter, as in all Catholic countries. But many women still conceived before marriage and some gave birth to children out of wedlock.

In England from the eighteenth century onwards it has been estimated that as many as one third of the brides were pregnant at marriage.[28] Pre-marital pregnancy is obviously linked to the age of marriage, as Malthus pointed out; in India or in Africa there were few children by unmarried mothers since girls were usually married by the age of sixteen.

In France a Revolutionary law of 1793 had established parity between natural and legitimate children who became equal regarding rights to inherit (the right to support already existed) and there was to be no attempt to discover the biological father. Under the more conservative Napoleonic Code of 1804, natural children were no longer able to inherit, although the prohibition on searching for paternity was retained since there had been some scandalous cases of false claims under the Ancien Régime. There was also the fear of infanticide or that women would abandon a child rather than reveal the name of the father.

The consciously-felt dilemma of the old Poor Law was one experienced by all welfare, namely, the danger of providing a disincentive to work and of promoting a culture of dependency. The scale system, under which family earnings were automatically made up to a certain minimum, became seen as placing the industrious labourer at a disadvantage compared with the indolent; 'the actual earnings became a matter of indifference' both to the worker and to the employer. Women's earnings were usually deducted from the allowance, so that they were disinclined to work except clandestinely. Where this was not the case, they might work while their husbands drew the dole, leading some to write of 'the rapid demoralization of the labouring classes', accompanied by 'an alarming increase in rates'.[30] At the same time people were conscious of another dilemma. It was recognized in the sixteenth century for example that to maintain illegitimate children might encourage fornication, while to refuse such support might promote either infanticide or abortion. The provision of support was usually the preferred course of action but the problems were recognized.

Secularization

Given that Christianity had such a significant influence on the structure of the European family, the process of secularization was bound to relieve the pressures from this source and so transform the order of things. As has been remarked, the great change in the intellectual climate between the early modern period (say, 1500) and today is that the former 'contained the notion of a world in which the Devil, demons and evil spirits were omnipresent'. [30] The same was almost as true of God.

Christianity was not the only religious force in Europe nor was it by any means monolithic. So-called 'heresies' took different views on family matters, as did other religious sources which included Islam in Spain, Sicily and in eastern Europe, as well as Judaism throughout the continent. Both of these allowed much closer marriages, including those of a leviratic kind. Moreover, powerful as it was Christianity did not have all its own way. Family pressures in favour of close marriages manifested themselves throughout the period of its dominance, sometimes by evasion, sometimes legitimized by dispensation.[31] There was always some resistance against the Christian rules precisely because they resulted in the alienation of family wealth.

When the dominance of religion in social life began to decline, with the New Learning of the Renaissance and later the Enlightenment, pressures to conform eased considerably. Secularization implies the abandonment of supervision by the church and the adoption of this role by the state. Foucault saw this happening in the late eighteenth, early nineteenth centuries. 'Sex became a matter that required the social body as a whole . . .' The process can be seen as the substitution of one form of policing by another as a result of the Enlightenment following on what Weber referred to as the demystification of the world. But this was not the first time that secular powers had intervened in family matters as some proponents of 'modernization theory' have imagined; that happened during the Renaissance and the Reformation and had been common enough in the classical world. But it was new to post-medieval Europe when by and large domestic life had fallen under the aegis of the church, as in other world religions. In Catholic countries the church continued to claim greater authority than the state.[32]

Such rival claims had led to many earlier conflicts of interest, culminating in England in Henry VIII's rejection of papal authority and the redefinition of the marriage rules. The struggle continued. The French king refused to agree with the Council of Trent's acceptance of marriages that had not received parental approval. Much later in Italy, the newly established nation of the 1870s engaged in a fierce battle with the Catholic church which had refused to recognize its legitimacy. The parliament in return required all marriages to be civil ceremonies, no longer accepting those conducted by the church and bastardizing the children of such unions just as much earlier the church had attempted to do with customary ones.[33] So the ratio of illegitimate children increased after Unification, but in fact in 40 per cent of cases the father's name was registered, indicating that a religious marriage had probably already taken place.

One aspect of this process of secularization affected the notion of diabolic possession, usually of young women, which virtually disappeared by the later eighteenth century, as did that of exorcism since most Protestants discounted the priest's role in this. By the late seventeenth century witchcraft ceased to be a major social problem, which it had earlier been in the mid-fifteenth century despite the church. Both Catholics and Protestants accepted its existence, which was seen to be an expression of heresy. But as the seventeenth century progressed, more members of the educated elite began to question not the existence of a power for evil but whether those accused were truly in contact with that power.[34] Both French and British judges began to mistrust the accusers, while the Inquisition started to turn the tables on the witch-hunters. By the end of that century the growing rationalism of the educated encouraged the abandonment of persecution.

In England in the eighteenth century there was also a decline in the importance of ecclesiastical courts, combined with a growing disinterest of justices of the peace in adultery or immorality, unless the expense of maintaining a child threatened to fall upon the poor rates. So that there was 'a decriminalization of sexual relations outside marriage'.[35] That was all part of a gradual separation between ecclesiastical and state regulations with the latter becoming increasingly central for the bulk of the population. This secularization can be seen very clearly in the gradual acceptance of the possibility of the remarriage of divorced men and women, still forbidden by some congregations but made possible under government auspices.

Like Protestantism, the Counter-Reformation was concerned to promote education which with the New Learning had been increasingly released from religious control, encouraging a more secular view of the world, especially in the natural sciences, although this was always segmental. But a related aim of the Counter-Reformation was to educate the parish priest in the views of the church and to bring him more closely under the control of the hierarchy. In this way he was expected to promote its values. In the words of one scholar, he was to teach his parishioners the 'new concept of family and of female honor; he was no longer . . . the link between the faithful and the sphere of the sacred, but between the faithful and the ecclesiastical and civil authorities'. In this he was aided by what have been refered to as his 'female spies'.[36] The papal police, too, played their part in upholding morality, seeing it as their duty to break up adulterous couples.

This present chapter has tried to point to some of the broader influences which the religious changes of the sixteenth century had on marriage and the family, in doctrine and often in deed, influences which in certain respects drew a line between the Catholic and Protestant areas that began to close only when mass secularization and the impact of full industrialization made themselves felt and then perhaps only with the Third Industrial Revolution after the Second World War and the emergence of the European Community.[37] So in pursuing this theme I have not always been able to stick strictly to chronological periods, as is also the case in the following chapter.

7

Dowry and the Rights of Women

As we have seen, one of the fundamental features of European marriage, from earliest classical times to the nineteenth century, has been the allocation of parental, occasionally other, property to women at marriage in the form of the dowry. Indeed it is one of those features that goes back not only to the Bronze Age societies of the Near East but is a widespread aspect of all the major Eurasian societies in stark contrast to those of Africa and other similar economies.[1] It constitutes part of what I have called the woman's property complex and it may supplement or act as an alternative to inheritance at death or to other forms of transmission between the living.

Dowry as Devolution

Dowry I have suggested should be seen as part of the process whereby property is transmitted between the generations; such devolution includes not only inheritance but also educational expenses, marriage transactions (including dowry) and other transfers between the living. Regarding dowry transactions, attention has been called to the different forms these may take and it is claimed that I see dowry as excluding women from inheritance. That is not the case.[2] I see both dowry and inheritance as part of an intergenerational process of devolution in which daughters have access to parental property.[3] Of course, it makes a difference if the property is handed down earlier rather than later. The problems involved I have discussed not only for inheritance (which I refer to as the King Lear situation) but also for succession to office (the Prince Hal situation).[4] Although often managed by the husband as part of a conjugal fund, the dowry continues to belong ultimately to the wife and her offspring, as we see in the arrangement made for her widowhood (dower, *douaire*) which were linked to the initial contribution made on her behalf. As has been emphasized for medieval London, marriage involved transfers to a 'partnership' (what I have called a conjugal fund) 'in which both partners and their families contributed capital and real estate to make a viable, familial, economic unit'. The announcement of the property exchanges and promises were made at the church door at the time of marriage, to secure ample witnesses.[5] When women lived longer than men after marriage, which they did especially with the later marriage for men from the fifteenth century, the widow received a dower of one third of the husband's estate for her life use. Widowhood gave her much greater legal and economic freedom. Her children too were provided for, the large majority being in the custody of their mothers, who frequently remarried when they were well-off. In sixteenth-century England one-third of widows remarried. In a class stratified society, families sought to preserve the status of daughters as well as of sons and therefore endowed them with property, usually less but sometimes more than their male siblings. Such transfers meant that they could try to make a 'match' within the same socio-economic group and so preserve the way of life of themselves and their offspring, as well as the reputation of their families. Marriage usually aimed to be within the same group rather than outside, although the Christian church insisted that close kin (sometimes most kin) should be excluded as potential partners.

Marriage of Heiresses

Restrictions on the marriage of women were strongest when they were heiresses, that is brotherless daughters who were eligible to inherit under the widespread Eurasian practice of direct inheritance, whereby property passed to the offspring, both females and males, before going to any collaterals (siblings or their children). Heiresses were of course particularly attractive as spouses and their wealth made it possible for them to bring husbands sometimes from lower groups or younger sons from upper ones, to come and live with them rather than their having to move to the husband's house, as in ordinary marriages. Under the demographic conditions that obtained some 20 per cent of couples might at the end of their lives find themselves with female rather than male heirs; as a consequence the heiress often played a dominant role in important spheres of family life.

One way of keeping family property in male hands was of course by adoption, but we have seen this was ruled out by the church, effectively in favour of the rights of daughters (and in effect of itself). The same applied to collaterals. The banning of the alternative (male-centred) strategies of heirship by the church meant that greater emphasis was placed on the transmission to brotherless daughters. That remains true today where rural property is particularly affected.[6]

Women Endowed

The fact that brotherless daughters inherited as heiresses before male collaterals must perhaps qualify some current views about the fate of women. In the sixteenth century Bologna is described as a 'patrilineal society' in which 'the entire inheritance went to the sons, minus the considerably smaller share used to endow daughters, either for marriage or for the nunnery'.[7] That of course is a very considerable qualification to the notion of 'the entire inheritance' going to sons, since the dowry was not everywhere smaller than the son's share. And in any case with the 20 per cent of couples who died with no direct male heirs, it was daughters who inherited 'entirely'. Moreover such endowments are intrinsic to the system which aims at 'a union between economic and social equals' both in upper-class families and among the peasantry; endowment is a major mechanism for accomplishing a measure of 'class' in-marriage.

One historian writes of the High Middle Ages in Europe (1150–1309) in the following terms: 'most brides came with a dowry from their family and received a smaller marriage gift from their bridegroom or his parents. These two parts together made up a marriage portion [conjugal fund] which, after the death of the husband, provided for the care of the widow. The administration of the portion was entrusted to the husband who, however, could act only with the consent of his spouse and her friends. After the husband's death, also, a widow was often appointed manager of the estate until the children reached majority. To recuperate her portion, a widow had precedence over all other creditors of an estate'.[8] They were hardly without rights.

Women, Endowment and the Church

Such transfers continued to structure the majority of European marriages until recent times. In the early days of Christianity, as has been suggested by Gibbon and others, it made rich widows a potential object of attention by ecclesiastics who wanted to accumulate funds for the church. The teachings of canonists and theologians defended the wife's right to dispose of non-dotal assets as she wished, 'in particular for the purpose of pious donations and bequests'.[9] Such attention led in turn to protests by the families and by the state, but it continued to occur, especially in Catholic countries, until recent times.

These extensive ecclesiastical institutions had to be supported by endowments or gifts. The problematic involvement of the spiritual community in the alienation of family property was a continuing aspect of Christianity as can be seen from the analysis of Jesuit fund raising.[10] The order started in totally rejecting worldly goods for themselves, but since they were devoted to rechristianization and conversion the Jesuits discovered that they needed funds to acquire buildings and run an educational programme. So successful were they in this endeavour that 'this funding process . . . represents one of the largest private money-raising processes ever undertaken'. It came to be carried out very professionally, especially in their approach to widows. A married woman's dowry in patrician families in Italy in the sixteenth century was worth up to 20 per cent of the family's assets. This sum came under the husband's management but had to be invested to produce an income for the wife, of which she would have some for spending herself. That income she could use as well as non-dotal sums (for example, inheritance from relatives) for gifts, including ones to the church. As a widow she had much greater control and she could use her wealth to assist a priest, the 'father-confessor' on whom she often depended, sometimes in ambiguous ways; 'at the pivot of women's giving was a relationship between herself and her confessor'. That relationship did not go uncontested by families, who might imply an element of forbidden sexuality. In fact the hierachy sometimes had to intervene to restrain their own representatives. At Bologna the Gozzelini family considered itself particularly abused by the influence of the Jesuits over their women and the order there considered it prudent for a time to avoid legacies. Ignatius Loyola was concerned to reconcile the need for money to Christianize the world with the desire for good relations with the powerful. That was not always possible, leading to ambivalence towards the order and to its occasional expulsion, as from Venice in 1606. The vulnerability of the family fortunes fostered resentment. As a result, there existed an often fraught relationship between the funding of good works and family interests. It is probable, as some commentators have remarked, to interpret this problem in purely materialist terms. The history of the Jesuits shows that to be a limited interpretation of the impact of 'great organizations' such as the Christian church, whose spiritual activities necessarily altered family relationships partly because of the material demands. Both bequests and objections repeat events at the end of Antiquity and throw light on the continuing needs of the church and the demands it made, the contributions given, against family interests.

Dowry and Class

The amount and even the possibility of dowry is related to class. The poor had little to offer, for the dowry was normally provided by the bride's parents; however in some cases an indirect dowry might be supplied by the parents of the groom or by some charitable foundation (often the church in Catholic countries) or else acquired by self-accumulation, that is, with the girl going out to work, saving her earnings and accumulating her own trousseau. Since it takes time to save in this last way, that process is clearly associated with a later marriage age for women and with the establishment of a certain measure of independence from their parents. With an earlier age of marriage, this mode of saving for a dowry would disappear, possibly leading to an increase in the number of informal unions.

In poorer families even provision by parents might be linked to the adolescent working for them, just as bridewealth is similarly linked for a boy in West Africa. That provision was supplemented by 'pin-money' (referring to the process of packaging pins in paper, which was a source of personal income) carried out in one's spare time for an outsider such as a merchant. But a more secure way was to work outside the home on a long-term basis with the aim of saving money to establish oneself in marriage. One of the points that an analysis of kinship among the propertyless classes of western Europe in the nineteenth century brings out is that while there was little property to hand down, it was 'a common lower-class practice' for daughters to earn their own dowry.[11] However, parents did contribute to the costs of apprenticeship and schooling, in other words to educational expenses, in which they were sometimes helped by other kinsfolk. Self-accumulation was certainly one aspect of the European (especially the northern European) practice of adolescents going out to work on other farms as 'in-living servants'. At one level this was a 'rational' way of allocating labour, since any farm could keep what work-force it needed and dispense with the rest. At the same time the adolescents accumulated savings for the future, as they did if they went to work in the towns either in service or elsewhere; that constituted a form of temporary labour migration. Many of the migrants were females. Many pre-industrial cities in Europe were composed predominantly of women, often in service (whereas in African towns men are in the majority).

Leaving Home

Girls would leave home as early as 12 to 14 years, sons two years later. The demand for girls in dairying was especially strong in livestock areas. With the development of manufactures in the late seventeenth century, employers came to the country looking for cheap labour and to be near the sources of raw materials and of water power, so that alternative forms of local employment increased, especially for women, although opportunities in brewing and the preparation of food had long existed. The increase in such employment, together with putting-out and cottage industry more generally (in other words, proto-industrialization), tended to keep children at home and possibly encouraged the substitution of work training for dowry, as in the towns. The parents trained daughters to do a job, and benefited from their labour before they left home.

Roman Law and Common Law

There was a difference between societies under Roman law and those who followed common law. The first decreed 'let no marriage be found without a dowry as is possible', whereas under customary law there was greater flexibility, the principle being 'dote qui veut', 'endow who wishes'. While the first was carefully recorded by a notary in 'le pays du droit écrit', the country of the written law, under the common law a record was made only in cases of strict settlement among the aristocracy.

Disappearance of the Dowry

The greater flexibility of common law practice may be associated with the fact that among urban workers in some northern countries such as England, the dowry tended to disappear earlier, being replaced by the notion, already existing in the poorer classes, of providing children with the education and training needed for work.[12] That change affected middle class practice but not until the end of the nineteenth century in England and some thirty years later in France. In many parts of southern Europe, especially in the rural Mediterranean, ethnographic reports show that dowry transactions continue to be important even in recent times as a way of establishing a married couple.[13]

Dowry and Violence

In this shift away from dowry there may also have been some consequences for marital violence. In northwest Europe, where dowry disappeared earlier, a husband is two to three times more likely to murder his spouse than is a wife; in Languedoc (and possibly more widely in the south) the opposite is the case. The motive behind murder given by rural wives in the south is the desire to repossess their dowry and then to remarry. The dowry 'often entailed deep resentment by a wife that her husband was misusing her and her property and that his removal would allow her to repossess what was her own'.[14] This shows that the dowry was recognized as her contribution to the conjugal fund. Dowry disputes also figure among premeditated murders by men and

Hufton reports cases where wives have been killed because they did not finally bring what had been promised at the wedding.[15] That kind of murder is not found in the north. It was not so much the voluntary nature of the northern dowry that made the difference but rather 'the premature emancipation of working-class couples in north-western Europe from a parent-donated dowry'.[16]

From several points of view women in the northwest seem to have been less exposed to the extremes of marital violence than were Mediterranean wives. They could circulate more freely outside the home, could bring court cases themselves and later on were less influenced by father-confessors, so that their expectations of equal treatment may have been higher.

Informal unions

In a dowry system, especially under Roman law, not all prospective partners could accumulate the necessary funds but instead they entered into an 'informal union'. Such unions were particularly likely to occur with servants working away from home and living in the relative anonymity of the town. As a consequence many children were born out of formal wedlock and their existence should lead us to modify the results of demographic analyses based on parish registers. In sixteenth-century England, one-fifth of rural children were conceived (not born) out of wedlock, less in the following century possibly because of the increase in clerical control in both Protestant and Catholic areas generally. That control gradually receded, especially in towns, and at the end of the eighteenth century in some French cities up to 17 per cent of births were out of wedlock. The estimates for both informal unions and non-marital births fluctuate considerably, depending upon the economic situation and upon political factors but it seems to have been particularly high in England after Hardwicke's Marriage Act of 1754 when it has been suggested that as many as half the unions in England were unregistered.[17]

Changes in the Portion

The dowry has been seen as becoming increasingly formalized in the sixteenth and seventeenth centuries when 'women became bearers of liquid wealth'.[18] With the woman's property complex they were always bearers of wealth (not always liquid but frequently mobile, of necessity; they moved, it moved) but the proportion of the family estate given to the bride, or demanded by the groom, varied and may at that period have risen above the rate of inflation, at least in upper groups. Higher dowries were likely to be more formalized but formality must also be a variable over time. It is doubtful if there was any unilineal development. Certainly at the end of the eighteenth century efforts were made in Spain to limit the amounts involved, as had happened elsewhere since the extent of wealth having to be handed over at marriage was a pre-occupation of the senior generation on many early occasions in European history.[19] In noble and other families the high level of the dowry may have led them to consider seriously the number and sex of their children, leading to a falling birthrate between the sixteenth and eighteenth centuries when the average dropped from four to two children. That meant a contraction of the time such women devoted to childbirth; in the French aristocracy at this time women had finished childbearing by the age of 25, giving themselves greater opportunity to pursue other interests, at court, holding salons and in general making France the paradise for (upper) women that the philosopher Hume and others perceived.

The Ecclesiastical Dowry

A related feature of Catholic countries was the number of girls going into convents, which demanded a dowry but often a smaller contribution than marriage itself. Before 1650 three-quarters of the daughters of the Milan aristocracy entered convents. That was exceptional; elsewhere in Italy the proportion was one-third, which still reduced considerably the total fertility rate and dowry expenditure for this class. In England that possibly did not of course exist after the Reformation; daughters were more likely to marry out of their class, although a varying number remained spinsters – in the British peerage as many as 25 per cent in the eighteenth century, again reducing not only fertility but endowments too. However, aristocratic spinsters were then taken care of on the family estate, reducing the available wealth. In middle-class households too there were large numbers of unmarried women, often literate, who went to work as teachers, governesses, housekeepers, or even as authors. Lower down the social hierachy spinsters might cluster together like poor widows to save on expenses, but they still suffered considerable distress and lived less long than married women.[20]

Critics of the dowry

While the economics of the dowry impinged upon the domestic decisions respecting women, that was mainly because they were recipients of wealth, sometimes more than their natal families (and at times too the church and state) thought they could bear. So that, in this and in other ways, dowry has not always been regarded as an unambiguous benefit to women. At the French Revolution some female reformers (and earlier too some religious ones like Arcangela Tarabotti in Venice in the 1640s) attacked the dowry system as a constraint on women. It is not clear what they would put in its place since they clearly wished women to acquire the property that Condorcet saw as the foundation of citizenship.[21] Rather they seem to be objecting to the management of these funds by their husbands.

Dowry then has been seen as limiting free choice and as constraining women in other ways, such as having to obey the wishes of their families. Some have seen it as linked with the maltreatment of women, as in the recent 'dowry deaths' of India. The latter problems generally arise when a dowry is thought to have been promised but does not materialize. As a result the bride may then be brutally treated.[22] However under certain circumstances (for example, that of 'the merry widow') the dowry which is settled on the woman but often managed by the man is a factor promoting her independence; in any case it gives her family a continuing interest in her fate. As for constraining the choice of partner, that is undoubtedly the case but such constraint is a feature not of dowry alone but of the whole socio-economic system of post-Bronze-Age societies that stratifies women as well as men; people are expected to marry within rather than without, like rather than unlike, either of their own volition or of that of their kith and kin. That is not to say that choice by partners, involving 'love', was not also a factor; as Hufton amply bears out, in most cases there was not a crude alternative between arranged and love marriages (the former 'traditional', the latter 'modern'), for parents would in general be ill-advised to ignore the wishes of the young and vice versa. Whatever the role of love insisted upon by some historians in the eighteenth century, money was still involved in marriages, especially among the aristocracy.[23]

Dowry and Divorce

What was the effect on the working of the dowry of the ban on divorce? One ancient historian notes that 'the women's property often gave Roman husbands an incentive to be attentive to their wives' wishes', since wealthy matrons could always divorce over-bearing husbands. There is no evidence that this was the case in later Europe, for example in Florence.[24] Wealthy wives might still 'wear the trousers' because of what they had brought to the marriage, especially if they were heiresses. But they could not exercise the threat of divorce itself until the present century.

Marital Contracts

Many marital contracts in south Italy, which in the eighteenth century often included the provision of a home (or of rent) by the bride's parents, note that the items provided constituted part of her inheritance, and a few specify that she renounce any further claim on the patrimony.[25] As has been remarked, the *dote* for southern Italy was 'a settlement' and the property received was hers, though it came under the husband's administration.[26]

The provision of such a settlement required a great deal of planning ahead, as has been observed for Locorotondo in Apulia, more so than in the case of inheritance.[27] Marriages required the accumulation of property to establish the new couple, in varying degrees of independence. As a consequence, marriage was often delayed so that the senior generation could organize the property transfer to both women and men. In general one would expect societies that gave large dowries, that is, with a woman's portion being roughly proportional to a husband's or a brother's wealth, to have later marriage, even when the bride and groom were not responsible for contributing to their own endowments, though that was not always the case.

Dowry: Movable or Immovable?

It was not only the transmission of property to women and the timing of the transfer that was important but the nature of that property. In the case of an heiress the total estate was involved, including land and houses. But in other instances too women's dowry or inheritance might or might not include immovable property, with each possibly having very important consequences for social life. It seems to have been general in Apulia that women passed on urban houses to their daughters, and in these communities female solidarity was strong.[28] Meanwhile the old were looked after by their locally-resident daughters, potentially a more caring alternative to male-centred transmission. The link between care in old age, intergenerational settlements and pre-mortem gifts was clear in late medieval society and remains so in Mediterranean society today; it is a feature of most earlier societies without all-encompassing welfare provisions.[29] A change in the pattern of post-marital residence occurred in Apulia in the nineteenth century with fathers building places for sons in the country close to their own, a change associated with the intensification of agriculture demanded by the cultivation of vineyards. These were mostly day labourers and the pattern contrasted with the small proprietors of Calabria where the neighbourhood pattern was virilocal. The difference here was basically to do with the system of production which was central to family property. In Cyprus one finds the opposite trend, a move from transmission of houses to sons to transmission to daughters in order to attract proper husbands for them.[30]

The inheritance of houses by women obviously led to a measure of insecurity for widowers should their wives die before them. But in the much more likely case of the man dying first, the widow gained a great deal of security and did not find herself at the mercy of sons or step-sons, as she might in the opposite case.

The combination of dowry and dower has been related to the formation of the larger seigneurial ensemble, and particularly to its characteristic, what has been called the compensatory impartible mode of land devolution.[31] It is true that the dowry can often be regarded as a compensation for the woman being excluded from the inheritance of land, but the impartible or male-linked inheritance of land is only one possibility and dowry, both in land and in other forms of wealth, exists in many parts of Eurasia in the absence of a seigneurial system (but not I think in the absence of complex land-based or livestock-based differentiation). Unigeniture (of the European type) is never anything but partial; there is always some compensation for younger sons as well as for women. Too close a link is made if one does not look comparatively enough.

Dowry and the Position of Women

In generously acknowledging my work Seccombe suggests that the conceptual framework 'renders an unduly positive impression of women's position in medieval families, minimising their oppression'.[32] I do not think I know of any simple way of assessing oppression, which certainly existed, at any particular time except in a comparative context. What I have argued is that any statement about the position of women must take into account the allocation to them of parental property, either as dowry or as inheritance. To see this as disinheritance is an error. This form of transfer is intrinsic to the system, not a temporary feature. Eleanor of Aquitaine provided an extreme example of what happened in a significant percentage of cases. It is essential to see intergenerational transactions as a totality and to understand gifts between the living (*inter vivos*), like inheritance, as part of the overall process of devolution which in a dowry system is 'diverging'. It is true that at marriage the husband often takes control of his wife's property, sometimes 'illegally' so, but the ownership becomes clear in the case of divorce. With the husband's death, the widow controls a dower of one third of his estate. I am not arguing that these arrangements are not 'oppressive'; I am rather pointing to the difference with other types of society (for example, African cultures) in which women have no access to male property at all. The fact that in complex stratified societies they do is in my opinion related to the attempt of parents (not only fathers) to maintain the status of daughters as well as of sons.

It is the case that in England (as distinct from some parts of southern Europe) land was normally inherited by sons, in the landed aristocracy by entail. But cash dowries could be used to rent or buy land where there was a market. Secondly I have tried to make the point that in these systems brotherless daughters inherit land and chattels before the more distant males whom one might expect to benefit in a dominantly patrilineal ('patriarchal') system.

I do not see, as some do, women's property as being a breach of the 'patriline', a notion that I do not understand in this context, much less that of the 'conjugal patriline'.[33] If a woman inherits part of Aquitaine from her parents, or other property is bought in by her mother, it seems a curious inversion to regard this as a matter of the father's rather than the mother's line.

In conclusion the existence of dowry in Europe, and in Eurasia generally, was a central aspect of the family system, related to class differences that were relevant to women as well as to men. It structures the whole problem not simply of choice of partner but of the position of women throughout the marriage, especially after the death of the husband when widows often came to control what, in gross, was considerable wealth and which in earlier times they often channelled to the church. Wealth of course is not to be translated directly into authority and even power, but it makes an important contribution. In general dowry represented an empowerment of women.

8
The Differences

Europe is by no means homogeneous in its family systems, despite the common factor of the Christian religion persisting over a millennium and a half. Earlier differences undoubtedly affected later practices, though not in the radical manner that some 'Germanists' have proposed. Later there were the incoming minorities bringing their own practices; Jews continued to follow many Old Testament rules that the Christians had modified, although the informal pressures and national laws of the host communities often led the immigrants to adapt; Muslims, whether invaders or converts, in Spain, southern Italy and eastern Europe also maintained (or adopted) Near Eastern practices in a determined way.[1] The nomadic gypsies (Roma) developed their own distinctive patterns related to their mode of livelihood. Equally class differences have been fundamental to all European societies and I have tried to discuss these throughout this essay. But the two major axes of difference in Europe I want to deal with in this chapter are firstly that between the main Christian denominations, especially in post-Reformation times, and secondly that variously characterized as North and South, or Northwest and the Rest, and sometimes as West and East. The second relates to the divide that demographic and other historians have seized upon in recent years, mainly in an attempt to account for the dominance of the northwest in the development of industrial capitalism in Europe (but certainly not of mercantile capitalism). That division partially overlaps with the areas of Roman and of common law, the former being essentially the country of '*le droit écrit*', of written law, the latter of the customary variety. It is also sometimes linked to a division between western (or northwestern) and eastern Europe, as in discussions of the European marriage pattern, but this axis we will treat separately.

North and South

Let me begin with the age of marriage, which varied considerably over time and space but in the sixteenth century there was a broad difference between north and south Europe which seems to have largely disappeared by 1800. Earlier on, southern women tended to marry early and men later, whereas in the north the age of marriage was late for both. Brides, and wives generally, were younger in the south and therefore tended to be more constrained, repositories of the honour (or shame) of their families, leaving home earlier to go into marriage rather than into service, and initially were possibly in a less egalitarian position with regard to the husband and his family, since they were younger and had rarely been employed outside.

In the north the age of marriage for both men and women varied over time, depending upon prosperity. In bad years, the union was delayed and hence the onset of childbearing was later; in this way fertility was controlled. Sons often left the parental home as servants, unless they were heirs, and when they married they stopped that work and set up on their own. Daughters moved out later for marriage but earlier for work; whereas in the south, before 1800, earlier marriage for women meant moving into the husband's parental home until the time was ripe for the couple to set up on their own. Single household units were less common and the wife was more housebound, but she received greater support from affines, though that support might also make it more difficult to leave to escape a brutal husband, except violently.[2]

This difference, as we will see, has been related to the pattern of household formation and family life more generally but it has sometimes been characterized in terms of variations in the stress on patriarchy. That concept is not easy to pin down in any precise way. It has been noted that 'the strong patriarchal model of the prescriptive literature of church and state looks somewhat different when viewed in the perspective of real-life experience', of 'marriage-in-action'.[3] Nevertheless 'patriarchal control' is still seen as being stronger in the areas of Roman law where it was reinforced by an obligatory dowry and by the more explicit southern codes of honour and shame. But even in those southern areas, there was more complementarity in marriage (less 'patriarchal' dominance) than the written codes allowed. Such complementarity was evident in aristocratic marriages, whether at court or in the country, among the middle class, among artisans, and especially perhaps in those rural regions of France, such as the Rouergue and Aveyron, where the seasonal migration of men to harvest grapes or olives further south in Languedoc, as in the Abruzzi, was part of the necessary expediency of survival, leaving the women to cope with the farm and the family.

Less patriarchy, more complementarity in the north, have been associated with greater equality between partners (and even 'love' in the special sense that they could, especially when working outside the home, make their own choice of a mate) as well as affection between parents and children; in other words, in the eyes of many historians and sociologists we have the embryo of the modern family living in smaller households. However, there is little evidence that children in larger families are any less cared for than in smaller ones, except in terms of *per capita* expenditure and of adult attention, both of which however may affect education, for which there is always a considerable cost. And love in the sense of choice of spouse is largely a function of the age of marriage and the nature of the economy. When those change, so too does the question of choice.

The designation 'patriarchal' has been liberally applied not only to areas in the Alto Minho in Portugal and to those parts of southern Italy and Greece where women inherited the houses themselves (and therefore automatically defined the locus of the marriage), but also to the many cases of marriage throughout Europe where a husband moved into his wife's house when she was an heiress. The fact that these latter variations or modifications were not explicitly recognized in the code serves to remind us of the difficulty faced by those whose evidence is largely confined to the written word. Was it that 'the patriarchal family needed to be given the force of law'?[4] Or was the written code more patriarchal (as in Ancient Rome) than the family itself? If the patriachal family was so strongly entrenched as is suggested, legal backing would surely be unnecessary. And what was the alternative to patriarchy, given that so wide a range of relationships seem to be included in this term?

However, there is certainly more emphasis placed upon concepts of honour and shame in the south as compared with the north, a difference that often centres upon the chastity of women and upon the reputation of their male defenders, which resulted in more careful supervision.[5] This feature may be at the basis of what an American observer called in a much-criticized phrase the 'amoral familism' of the south (which comprised extended 'families', the Mafia, and in general a greater degree of local control).[6]

It was less easy to supervise the children of those northern families who were working away from home at an early stage. For instance working away drastically reduced the element of the parental say in marriage choice. That interference constantly took place in the upper echelons of society where marriage involved larger redistributions of property. But if young men or women were working elsewhere and accumulating their own savings, there was little to prevent them marrying whom they wished, as has been argued for France; such freedom was more difficult to find in southern countries like Italy or Spain where until the eighteenth century women married earlier, men later, and daughters tended to be more carefully supervised and kept within the (extended) household.[7]

The contrast between Roman law in the south and customary law in the north emerges in the methods of inheriting property. The modes of inheritance vary considerably across Europe, often as alternative solutions to similar problems. But within France considerable and regular differences between north and south seem to be related to the presence or absence of Roman law.[8] The North followed some form of partible inheritance whereas the South followed written Roman law and was precipatory, that is, the father could appoint a single heir, usually the eldest son but sometimes the first to marry, and on this marriage he handed over control of the farm, the *oustal*. The Revolution of 1789 attempted to change all that and on 7 March 1793 the National Conventions decreed that all offspring enjoyed equal rights. Modifications were later made in this decree which was intended as an attack on the political threat of noble primogeniture. But the peasantry in the south were deeply disturbed (except for some younger sons) and sought ways of circumventing the law. 'By refusing to withdraw their portions, by accepting quite ludicrous valuations, by remaining celibate or by migrating into Holy Orders, less favoured offspring acquiesced in their own disenfranchisement and in so doing paid homage to the values represented by the *oustal*.[9] There is plenty of evidence to show that many peasants accepted the logic of the stem-family and the impartible inheritance strategy that buttressed it; that situation continued to persist throughout the nineteenth century, indeed until today.

This inheritance of the *oustal* affected the composition of the household; in 1876 in the *bourg* of Sauveterre in the Ségala, a quarter of the households contained a couple with offspring plus a member of the senior generation. In that same area in the 1880s an English traveller noted that 'the parents work incessantly to build up a home . . . and when the eldest son or daughter marries they give up that home to the young couple with whom however, they continue to live, always working'.[10]

Differences in family structure between the north and south of Europe, between the Mediterranean and the trans-Alpine regions, have continued to mark the continent, as can be clearly seen from the statistics collected by the European Union. Divorce is today less common in the south, as are cohabiting unions and illegitimacy, a fact that may be partly related to the greater commitment to Catholic religious norms. However, other differences do not go in the same direction, running contrary to earlier trends. Fertility is today lower in Italy and in Spain than in their northern counterparts, and seems to be associated with the adoption of later marriage (possibly as a transitional feature) and with the longer residence of children (especially males) with their parents, partly as the result of high unemployment.

Later marriage is also linked to the efforts made by prospective partners in these countries to endow themselves with the increasing amount of expensive goods seen as necessary to start a new household, an endowment which may take some time to build up. Late marriage in the northwest has been seen as an important way in which that region controlled its fertility; today this propensity is greater in the south, suggesting that these variables are much more contingent, less deeply 'cultural', than many have supposed.

The north–south differences are confounded with two others; firstly, with the opposition between northwest Europe and the rest (including the east outside the continent) insisted upon in accounts of the European marriage pattern, which is seen to be related to the achievements of those areas in developing capitalist activity; and secondly with the difference between Protestant and Catholic countries. Once again a north–south, or west–east divide is, in the view of Weber and other sociologists and historians, linked by 'elective affinity' to the same process.

That view is very prevalent. For example, an early modern historian has recently seen the 'unique marriage pattern' of pre-industrial Europe, with a late age of marriage for both men and women, a substantial proportion of never-marrieds and nuclear households with living-in servants, as helping to 'explain the economic divergence between industrialising western Europe and the rest of the world in the nineteenth century'.[11] While that 'unique pattern' might accompany economic divergence, that it explains such activity is a quite different and disputable proposition.

The contrast between the northwest and the rest of Europe was part of a wider contrast between western Europe, the assumed home of capitalism, and the rest of the world in terms of the mean size of household, which reflected the paucity of three-generational households associated with the early departure of adolescent children to work elsewhere, their later age of marriage and the frequency of non-marriage (that is celibacy). However, mean size of households turns out to be a poor measure of difference and one of the main proponements of this argument, Hajnal, subsequently pursued his analysis in terms of the formation rather than the composition of households. The search for major differences in the size of households (MSH) between West and East was now abandoned; Russia, for example, has been found to have units much larger than India, 9.1 as compared with five in the so-called joint-family households of India, which approximates to the figure for northwestern Europe on which so much has been built (the 'small, isolated, nuclear family').[12] The focus has now shifted to the internal structure of domestic groups, and specifically to the process of household formation. Hajnal distinguishes two main forms which again emphasize an east–west divide; the 'joint household (formation) system' of the major Eurasian societies on the one hand is contrasted with the northwest European system on the other. The latter is based on late marriage for men (over 26) and women (over 23), and on the move of a proportion of those men and women before marriage to work for others, often as in-living life-cycle servants.

In 'joint household systems', on the other hand, both men and women marry early and live jointly with the husband's parents, so that two or more couples inhabit the same dwelling unit. In fact the difference is by no means absolute in terms of structure. In a contemporary Maharastran sample, 77 per cent of households were not joint (that is, did not have two couples); in the Danish sample referred to earlier (p. 65) the figure was 93.4 per cent.

If people marry early in predominantly agricultural societies, marriages are more likely to be 'arranged', whereas with later marriage, men and women going into service can save to help set up their own households and are freer to choose their partners. Nevertheless there is little difference in household size since in both cases fission occurs but at slightly different times. Joint households of more than one married sibling tend to split before or shortly after the father's death, whereas the others divide, in effect, at the time of the marriage of the children. Each type of household undergoes fission, so that in the two systems similarities exist in the ages of their heads: when the split occurs, a new head of a joint household is generally about 30, not much older than the average marriage age for a man in northwest Europe.[13]

The northwest European pattern of household formation is seen as linked not only to life-cycle servanthood, late marriage, independent post-marital households, but with retirement contracts for the senior generation and public provision for the poor. The implication often drawn from public provision is that, as with life-cycle service (the participants in which remained unmarried), Europe had some special key that held fertility in check and so contributed to economic development. But public assistance to the poor was a widespread feature of the major Eurasian societies which also had other ways of controlling population growth.

This set of factors constituted for Hajnal a household formation system that 'arose only once in human history'. Of any cluster of weighted variables one can make a similar claim and it seems difficult to consider this cluster as unique in that respect, one capable of being invented only once and which affected the unique development of western capitalism. That is to make ethnocentric claims that do not seem sustainable.

For the differences with southern European families, the contrast used by members of the Cambridge group was between the small households of western Europe and the larger ones of Tuscany in the fourteenth and fifteenth centuries. The work on the Florentine cadastre brings out two main features, a low female marriage age and a high incidence of multiple-family households.[14] The effect of this finding is to loosen the connection between the northern European family and 'modernization' because as business historians have argued it was precisely in this part of Italy that the main features of merchant capitalism developed in Europe (similar developments took place elsewhere in Eurasia). Such developments were not inhibited by the early marriage of women nor yet by larger households. In any case the Mediterranean was by no means uniform with regard to these demographic features.

For recent work shows that these conclusions about the age of marriage are inadequate, as they are for the Iberian peninsula.[15] Italy demonstrates great internal variation. In Venice in the eighteenth century the marriages of both males and females were delayed, up to 30 years of age for men and 29 for women. In southern Italy men married at 23 and women at 20. While in fifteenth-century Florence marriages were early, in rural Tuscany in the eighteenth century women could marry at 25 or even 27; nevertheless people often lived in multiple households even though the so-called 'non-European' pattern of marriage had disappeared by the mid-seventeenth century. As the age of marriage grew later, complexity increased.

Regarding service, in northern Italian cities in the sixteenth century up to one-half of men and one-third of women spent several years in the households of other people, though the figure was less in rural areas. But that situation changed radically in the seventeenth century and after, when there were fewer servants and those largely female. Some service continued in rural areas but in southern Italy the pattern was quite different, there being few servants except in Sardinia, which was also characterized by late marriage and a greater role for women. It has been suggested that the late marriage and the large number of servants in Sardinia was due to the fact that children were expected to accumulate their own dowry before marriage by working outside the home. Certainly the two features may be related, as we have seen. The age gap between men and women was close and the position of the latter was more favourable. Unlike the rest of Italy, a woman had the same rights as a man to share in the paternal estate; elsewhere they got only an early portion as a dowry. It may be that, as in other communities where men work away, Sardinian women played a greater role in the family than Sicilian ones because in the pastoral economy the men were so often located in encampments in the mountains.[16] Another explanation of late marriage for men and women in Sardinia, as for neolocal residence and life-cycle servanthood, was its 'individualistic' nature, though this concept, thought to be more appropriate for the north, is less than satisfactory.[17] Interestingly it has been Italian scholars who have offered the most incisive

critiques of the work of the demographic historians of the northwest in an attempt to refine those models and show that much of
Italy (for example the northern cities) was not 'non-European'.[18]

However, fifteenth-century Florence does approximate to the
'non-European' pattern, which continued longer among the bourgeoisie. In the rural south neolocal residence and the nuclear family
predominated, as in the north, but there was little outside domestic
service since women married young. On any reckoning, Italy was
of fundamental importance in the growth of the mercantile
economy in Europe as well of the Renaissance itself; there is,
however, little correlation of such developments with the selected
demographic variables which varied throughout the country.

Eastern Europe

Let me turn to the differences between west and east Europe which
have been seen as approximately parallel to those between north
and south. The east is said to have had 'a non-European marriage
pattern', with earlier marriages, less celibacy, larger households (or
a different system of formation). Ecological factors are also relevant here. Eastern Europe was much less densely populated than
the west. During the eighteenth century, countries like Italy, the
Netherlands and Belgium had more than 46 persons per square
kilometre, while Britain, Spain and central Europe ran between 15
and 46. But southeastern Europe had fewer than 15. In the first
half of the nineteenth century, the average population density of
the Balkans was 13.4 per square kilometre, while for the whole
of the Ottoman Empire it was 10.5. Low density and mountainous terrain are connected with pastoral or mixed agriculture,
which in turn encouraged larger domestic groups, one use of the
word *zadruga*; another use of the word related to military settlements or to the larger households on estates where sharecropping
or the corvée was required.[19] All these situations placed a premium
on having more than one male per household to provide the
additional labour.

However, it would be dangerous to exaggerate these differences
as many have done in taking western Europe as their original focus
and as seeing the Balkan *zadruga* and the Russian *mir* as evidence
of a long-standing (and more 'primitive') collectivist spirit among
these peoples. In the first place we know little about the earlier
history of the *zadruga*, which is a nineteenth-century literary

concept. When we examine this idea there seem to be more specific reasons for its appearance in an area in which in fact the predominant form is the small household. 'The major distinction', it has been said, 'between the West European family and the Southeast Europe (or Balkan) one lies not so much in the quantitive differences, but rather in the fact that in the Balkans the extended and multiple-family type was more often and for a longer period a developmental stage of the individual family life-cycle.'[20] In other words the generations lived together for a longer time before a split took place.

Among all Bulgarian confessions, Muslim and Christian (both Orthodox and Catholic), marriage was universal and early. In Russia that fact is connected with considerably larger households; in the region of Mishino in 1814, 78 per cent of households were multiple.[21] However, in Bulgaria simple households predominated, although they were not necessarily independent economically and socially (as Sabean showed for Germany and as was widely the case in other rural areas). Marriage consisted of two stages, the engagement and the wedding. The first included the negotiations for the marriage prestations, in which there was a parental fee (or *agarlik*) said to be seen as a compensation to the bride's family.[22] In Muslim marriages there was also a sum allocated by the groom's family to the bride which she received if her husband died or left her, a common Near Eastern arrangement.[23] The bride might also receive jewelry or even a field or vineyard which the husband could not reclaim. In addition she was given a direct endowment from her parents, consisting of clothing, household goods and very often money, cattle and even real estate. This was her dowry, direct and indirect, that eventually passed to her children, in some places only to her daughters.

The age of marriage differed in rural and urban areas. In the 1860s the former was described as being very late for men and in the big towns there was a considerable number of bachelors. However, women married earlier than in western Europe, at about the age of 20 on the average, which compared to the 'Mediterranean pattern' as illustrated by the data on Tuscan cities, although there was a similar difference in the countryside. That difference occurs in both western Europe and Russia. In towns many men have to finish their specialist training and acquire a house before marrying; again training and self-accumulation delay the age of marriage.

It is possible that in parts of northwestern Bulgaria there existed,

into the thirteenth century, the practice of *snohachestvo*, the
marital cohabitation of the father-in-law with the daughter-in-law.
This feature of co-residence appears to have occurred when the
father was a widower and had a young son whom he married to an
older girl to 'light the oven' and perhaps act as his partner.
Marriage to older brides was not at all uncommon in some rural
areas. A local saying ran 'Where there is more property and less
people, they see to it that girls are older than boys'.[24] A similar
relationship with the daughter-in-law has also been reported from
Russia.[25] In the early nineteenth century 'an underage boy might be
married to an older girl for economic reasons, and she would
become mistress of her father-in-law (who was then called a
shokhach)'.[26] Such arrangements became less common with the
ending of serfdom in 1861 but restricted living space must always
have led to tension between father and daughter-in-law, meaning
that the notoriously hostile relationships between mother and
daughter-in-law were often tinged with sexual jealousy.

Westerners see such practices as manifestions of abuse; they can
be said to involve sexual exploitation (as perhaps all older–younger
partnerships), although in many cases the actual husband was
younger than his bride. It is more difficult to describe this relationship as abusive since it was institutionalized and presumably
anticipated if not necessarily welcome by the future bride.
However, she was not always without her own resources. The
Russian wife had no stake in her husband's property but she
had her dowry (*pridanoe*, which might include land and livestock)
and the fruits of her labours, which might be inherited by the
daughters.[27]

The practice of bundling, that we earlier associated with
Germanic societies, was also found in the Ukraine where young
men visited girls sleeping in haylofts in summer. The visit was
sometimes followed by a conception and there is some disagreement about whether this enhanced or damaged her marriage
chances, depending no doubt on whether the father wanted to
marry her.[28]

Part of eastern Europe did differ from the West in certain
important respects. Many households in Russia were similar to
west European ones and if there was surplus labour, children
certainly went out to work in the nineteenth century on other farms
or in factories. In the case of a couple having only daughters, a son-
in-law might be persuaded, as elsewhere, to move into his wife's
family house, making a filiacentric union. But there was a greater

tendency for men to marry earlier and for the young couple to begin life in the parental home.

Russia has been found to have a much larger mean size of household, which was not only higher than the rest of Europe but of India and China too.[29] It was distinctly 'non-Western'. Hajnal, as we have seen, regards the eighteen-century figures from Hungary as falling in the joint family range. In Neckarhausen in Germany houses frequently contained more than one married pair throughout the eighteenth and nineteenth centuries, averaging about 1.4 families. The difference is not all that great between 'joint family households' and others. In any case the differences in size and formation of households did not appear to make Russia any less welcoming to industrialization than other central European countries. For there the larger (expanded) households seem to be associated with the demands of the state: when one adult male was required for compulsory military service, another brother or perhaps a cousin remained to carry on with the farm.

As elsewhere, in earlier Sri Lanka for instance, the demands of the state or other authorities for a labour contribution encouraged larger households or dwelling groups; that was also the case in the hill farms of Albania where on the same farm male labour was required both for the valley fields and for herding in the uplands.[30] Ecology is an important influence on family life. The distribution of labour between the base and the schieling, or summer dwelling in the hills where pastures were more abundant, is a general feature of hill communities. Moreover such regions were more likely to be outside the reach of the state and therefore to have to make their own arrangements for collective defence, or attack, as with Scottish clans. So larger households or dwelling groups were not necessarily the sign of a 'backward' society incapable of adapting to change, but of a different ecology, way of life and political circumstances.

Catholic and Protestant

A number of recent writers have played down the effects of the confessional differences between Protestants and Catholics on marriage and the family at the time of the Reformation.[31] Reforms are seen as continuous with fifteen-century efforts in that direction. My argument has been that there was always tension between what the church decreed and what many families wanted and even practised in certain spheres, a tension that was visible in the activities of reformers and indeed often of the generality of people, well before the Reformation. But the later revision of 'the holy, indissoluble, and consensual' nature of marriage did have significant results, in weakening ecclesiastical authority over marriage by desacralizing the union, by rejecting the opinions of Councils that were in opposition to the written word of God and by loosening the authority of earlier ecclesiastical courts. In this way, it opened the gate to a more secularized version of marriage. In more specific terms, it made possible, at first in but a limited way, divorce and subsequent remarriage; it placed firm limits on spiritual kinship, at least as an impediment to marriage, and it drastically reduced the range of prohibited degrees, both consanguineal and affinal, as well as getting rid of the whole system of indulgences and dispensations. It also modified the notion of consensus in marriage, of clerical celibacy and indeed the whole complex set of monastic and lay orders that affected the histories of men and women alike (as Florence Nightingale forcibly pointed out), the strategies of families and the accumulation of property by Jesuits and others.[32] These factors all touched upon domestic life in various ways, including marriage and it seems short-sighted to pose the question largely in terms of the very broad aspects of marriage that tend to cross-cut not only Protestants and Catholics but most other sects and societies. In any case the confessional divide in Germany was of a particular kind, owing to the high degree of fragmentation of its political and religious regimes. One cannot imagine sharing churches or alternating bishops in New England, in Scotland or in Northern Ireland. Confessional differences became highly significant in those areas on a number of fronts, including the domestic.

In the previous chapter, I have remarked on the differences between Protestant and Catholic Europe, which links with my insistence on the religious dimension and on the support required by the Catholic Church to run a great organization. Protestants overturned the exclusive restrictions on marriage created by the Church, even allowing in the Anglican case (but not in the Calvinist) the unions of first cousins, though it took longer to permit the marriage to the dead brother's wife (since that prohibition Henry VIII had used to get rid of an unwanted spouse). In most Protestant communities divorce became no easier and the early attachment of Anabaptists to Old Testament practices such as polygyny was soon abandoned, although the Mormons held on to the custom longer until it was outlawed by the Government of the United States. In these spheres the Scriptures provided no long-term guide to those claiming to return to the Book.

There was some move among the Reformers towards emphasizing the greater responsibility of parents for children but that did not put a stop to the practice of wet-nursing which continued into the twentieth century.[33] However there was less institutional care for the children of unmarried mothers (single parents), more responsibility being placed on her and on the putative father. For convents had been abolished and there were now no longer the nuns to help run charitable homes and schools. Older women, especially widows, had a less organized social role to play in the community.

In Protestant countries there was initially the same explicit insistence on parental consent to marriage as in the practice of Catholic ones (which the Catholic Church tried drastically to modify). But from the mid-seventeenth century, debates gradually opened up the subject throughout Europe and the theme of choice by partner was taken up by many novelists, not only by the authors of 'romances' but by more significant writers like Richardson in *Clarissa*. However, a considerable gap remained between literature and reality, where choice was always hedged in by the 'boundaries of the appropriate'.[34] Parental influence 'perhaps bore a direct relationship to the amount of money they would put into a match, and whether the children were living at home . . .'.[35] That meant that aristocrats had to distinguish between long-term affection and family interest on the one hand, and 'short-term passion conducted within the ephemerality of the court'.[36] In other words between duty on the one hand and 'love' on the other.

Mode of livelihood

A number of differences within Europe are directly connected with the mode of livelihood. It has been suggested that sharecropping was associated with a proliferation of multiple-family households, due to the landowners' interest in maximizing the number of workers on the land, though that question is surely open to other solutions.[37] Some argue that the growth of wage-labour in agriculture in the eighteenth and nineteenth centuries led to people living in smaller, less complex family units. We have seen that the more prominent role of women in Sardinian life has been attributed to the pastoral livelihood where the man was absent for long periods and the same was the case in other situations such as in the fishing communities (of Catalonia or the North Sea), or where seasonal migration was practised by males as in the Rouergue and Aveyron.[38]

In the nineteenth century more women were employed in agriculture in France, more in domestic service in England; the difference reflected a difference in the economy, peasant farming being more important in the former. Women in France continue today to play a greater part in the external economy than in England. They contributed 34 per cent of the household income in 1981; in Britain in 1984 the comparable figure for working married women was 24 per cent.[39]

Some fifty years ago, the American sociologist George Homans followed up some suggestions of the French historian, Marc Bloch, and defined two systems of farming in western Europe in the late Middle Ages, that characterized by open-field farming, where individuals had claims to strips in communally-exploited fields, and the dispersed farms of the woodland champaign country.[40] In the former, individuals lived in nucleated villages and farmed one-man plots, so that younger sons had to remain as bachelors, marry 'heiresses' with rights to land, go off to 'assart', that is, open up new areas, or move to other occupations in towns or as migrant workers. Under these conditions households would tend to be smaller, kin scattered. In the champaign country, there was not the same restriction on the size of households; these could accommodate more relatives, or house them nearby. The effect on family relations of these two systems was far-reaching. Open-field systems tended to be associated with primogeniture, with only one son or child inheriting the indivisible plot, whereas the champaign woodlands were linked to partible inheritance which produced a more active market in land.

In the northern Italian countryside in the eighteenth and nineteenth centuries there were two main systems of agricultural exploitation, each of which affected the family in different ways. Where land was divided into small farms, whether owned or rented, the household constituted a single work unit and there was little female autonomy, though at times women worked in the fields along with men. They received a dowry at marriage but were treated equally regarding property only in so far as it was divided according to the Napoleonic Code, the provisions of which were confirmed by the post-unification Civil Code of 1865. Following those legal formations, women began to be allocated a share of the 'new patrimony', the acquired property, although the practice did not reach some distant areas until after the Second World War. Where rural families were only units of consumption and did not themselves have farms, women's autonomy was greater; they might work as day-labourers although at lower rates than men. Autonomy and freedom from constraints were often aspects of the lack of property as well as of the behaviour of some aristocrats who owned excessive amounts; 'class' was always an important dimension in the domestic life of the stratified societies of Europe, as of Asia.[41]

In sharecropping families in the north, a crisis at the beginning of the eighteenth century led to a deliberate effort to avoid 'proletarianization' by attempting to increase the masculinity of the workforce, delaying marriage and getting unmarried women to leave home. Sex ratios show considerably more men than women, with some of the latter going to work on other farms but more migrating to the towns which were mainly composed of females, as so often in Europe. Even widows moved, especially to textile centres. Indeed some employees built hostels near their factories to house the women, who might turn out to be the only member of the family to be earning money. If it was the men who moved to the factories, or emigrated further afield, the women often had to take over their farming tasks; as in wartime, there was a feminization of labour. In both these ways, women became increasingly independent.

There is of course much more to be said about the relationship between family and productive system, as will become clear in the final chapters. As with property (and its transfer to the church and other great organizations), the way of livelihood is fundamental to the understanding of the family, of differences and of changes. Here I have just used some examples as indicative of the early situation.

War and Revolutions

Finally I want to call attention to differences of another kind, initially limited in time, created by great upheavals, the effects of revolution and of war on the family. Revolutionary movements have often aimed to change radically the nature of family life, as have sectarian groups of a religious kind. That was the case in Europe with the coming of Protestantism. The dissolution of the Catholic church in Tudor England brought about a situation in which both the clergy and the people were confused about many of the norms of family life, in particular the restrictions on marriage which the church had instituted. Order was gradually re-established when the Elizabethan church invented and imposed its own rules. These were in some ways closer in spirit to the underlying wishes of the people, although they had also been subjected to scholarly and theological debate among the Reformers.

A secular equivalent of this revolution took place some 250 years later in France. From 1789, marriage was laicized in that the act of marriage no longer required a church service, although making a sacrament of marriage was not forbidden. The absence of the church service was not simply a question of ritual. Marriages that were validated by the state could also be undone. Divorce was not only possible but seen as a check on unions that were arranged by parents and forced on the couple. The whole system of inheritance changed; primogeniture was abolished in an attempt to weaken the power of landed elites and equal division was extended to daughters as well as to sons, throwing the southern countryside into a state of turmoil.[42] As in China (of 1911) and the Soviet Union (of 1917), revolutionary movements have sought to change family structure, as well as that of society more generally.

War has similarly transformed family life but unintentionally rather than deliberately. Some of the recent changes in the European family have been put down to the major wars that occurred in the first half of the twentieth century. Families have always been affected by war in ways that have been the subject of countless films and novels. War has dispersed its members, put the men in danger of death and the women at the risk of rape or prostitution. The latter increases dramatically when men are serving abroad and women having to make do on their own. In earlier times most European wars had relatively few participants, so the domestic effects were limited. In Russia, as we have seen, one man in a peasant household might have to join the army, promoting larger households and more communal arrangements with partners; military factors were undoubtedly related to the polyandrous arrangements of the Nayar of Kerala and of the Singhalese of Sri Lanka. But the religious wars of the Reformation involved much larger numbers and more widespread effects on domestic life, as Brecht's *Mother Courage* reminds us. Such effects have been particularly apparent in the two world wars of the twentieth century, leading to prolonged separation of couples, to the postponement of marriage and children, to the increase in adultery, prostitution and divorce, in fact to the decline in those values used to justify the war itself.

That is clear from the war-time situation in Italy and from the remedial measures that were taken at its end. During the war 'families had come under terrible strain as the men had gone away to fight and then to prisoner-of-war camps, women and young girls in the southern cities had . . . been forced into prostitution and children from the industrial North were separated from their mothers and sent into the countryside to escape the bombardments. The Italian family, as one priest wrote in early 1946 in *La Civiltà Cattolica,* had "undergone deplorable ruination and profanation".'[43] At the first Congress of the Christian Democrats in 1946, a leading politician made an appeal to his party to fight for the future of the Christian family; 'An invisible and silent atomic bomb has destroyed the family unit. The family, if it is not already dispersed, is more likely to unite around the radio . . . than around the domestic hearth.' Women especially should try to defend the family from the inside, against the state taking off husbands and brothers for war, and against atheist education and the corruption of the streets.

But changes were not only destructive. When men were away at war, women had long played a greater role in household, economic and even political affairs. In Ferrara, Eleanora of Aragon had run matters of state when her husband was absent as a *condottiere.* The same shift of gender control occurs in other circumstances when men are absent. Women formed a 'reserve army' in war-time situations. It was they who carried out many jobs otherwise done by males; while much of this employment was reversed with demobilization, the gendered division of work was nevertheless affected over the longer run; a model was established. In Basuto in Southern Africa, women take over the ploughing when the men are working in the mines; in coastal fishing communities they often play a prominent role, as they do in other situations of long-term or even short-term labour migration. Such conditions obviously reduce the part played by the husband with regard to the family as well as enhancing that of the women. During the Napoleonic wars when the men went off, there was more work for women and their role as a reserve army came to the fore opening up the possibility of change. Their skills as household managers were also sharpened; consumer goods were in shorter supply and prices rose – for example, that of bread. Shortages became pervasive, ingenuity was required to fill the gaps, but at the same time there was more work for those who remained behind.

It was certainly the case that the First World War hastened the advent of votes for women in the United Kingdom and of adoption in France; the first was directly related to the role women had played and the possibility was widely discussed in France, Ireland, Germany and elsewhere in Europe; the second related to the need to care for the children of those killed. At the same time the end of a war often saw pressure to return to earlier (family) values, to reinstate the pre-war state of affairs, as in much of Europe, not only Italy, after the Second World War. To some extent the radical movements of the 1960s, in their impact on interpersonal relations, represented a reaction against the reaction. The contradiction of the experience of war, and to some extent of revolution, was that it led to change even though peace also brought about an attempt to return to the earlier state of affairs.

In Europe we find many similarities in family life, as the result first of Christianity, then of widespread socio-economic changes and today of parallel trends and pan-European pressures. But there are also important axes of differentiation: class, religion, mode of livelihood and the geographical dimensions of East–West and especially North–South, with the Mediterranean providing many variations on common themes. But it is time to return to the common elements as they were influenced by socio-economic developments.

9
Proto and Full Industrialization

In earlier times the family in Europe was adjusted to two major and partly opposing factors, first the largely agricultural economy of a relatively advanced kind associated with plough agriculture and a range of post-Bronze-Age cultigens and crafts; secondly, the regulations of the Christian Church and its efforts to establish itself as a 'great organization'. Post Bronze Age societies were stratified in relation to land as well as having substantial mercantile and artisanal sectors, resulting in a series of different family constellations, and even 'non-family' ones such as the clergy, especially monks and nuns (modified in the Orthodox and Protestant Churches), the substantial body of bachelors and spinsters (usually living in a household), as well as of those who had once been members of a family (widows and abandoned wives, who sometimes did live alone). A counter value to the family is also reflected in the high number of children killed in infancy, in the West as well as the East.[1]

The numerically dominant element which has been at the centre of my discussion so far has been the rural family with access to land, though there were very important differences between rich and poor peasants. In addition we need to consider the seigneurial class as well as the landless.[2] Each of these groups followed variants of the strategies of marriage and heirship, linking people to resources, or to their absence. Meanwhile for merchants and for artisans the nature of those resources differed, and hence the familial relationships and strategies, since these were largely domestic enterprises. We get some idea of the differences in the urban contexts from accounts of Florence in the fifteenth century and of Ghent in the fourteenth.[3]

The Expansion of the Bourgeoisie and the Rural Proletariat

Those differences were exacerbated with the Renaissance. The consolidation of landholding meant larger numbers of landless workers and poor peasants in the countryside and a heavier migration to the towns. The development of trade, of services, of manufacturing activity and of the professional sector, including doctors and lawyers, saw the expansion of the bourgeoisie. So we find two important features that pointed to the future. On the one hand, there was the growth of the middle classes and the ever increasing importance of their family life and domestic norms; secondly, the proletarianization of much of the workforce took place as peasant agriculture ceased to occupy the same central role in the economy.

These developments occurred, in different degrees, in all the major Eurasian societies, as trade increased both within and between the major areas, that is, China, India and the Near East, then somewhat later in Europe when its economy experienced a rebirth during the later Middle Ages. As towns expanded, so too did the urban proletariat and the artisanal sectors. But much production, especially in the boyant textile area, took place in the country rather than the town with women playing an important part in diversifying the economy. In China domestic silk production fed into the export trade (along the Silk Roads) as well as into the huge internal market; from India cotton fabrics were exported early on to Indonesia and to Indochina well before they made their mark in the West where their emulation led directly to the mechanization of cotton production in the Industrial Revolution.

In Europe, too, the domestic production of textiles had long been part of mercantile activity. As in India that activity saw the development of putting-out, whereby merchants provided the goods for rural families to spin and weave, a development that became of increasing significance when people had reduced access to land and as the wider markets developed. That was part of the process of proto-industrialization which saw the proletarianization of part of the rural labour force. When early factories developed, using water power, they did so largely in the country, with the result that the way of life of many people changed dramatically, eventually leading to much increased migration to the factories in towns as the latter became more efficient for producing goods. That process in turn led to the development of the new urban working class.

This change in the economy was only one element in the situation regarding family formation. In the rural areas the 'traditional' family structure remained largely the same among the farming population. As has been observed for France, in that sector family life continued along similar lines.[4]

The aristocracy proceeded very much as before, though like others they were affected by the process of religious change and by the secularization of the family. But above all the development of the economy and of knowledge systems saw the great expansion of the middle class whose family norms became increasingly dominant throughout the society in tandem with the importance of that class itself. They were after all in basic control of the communication system through which these norms could be transmitted to other groups, for example, to the not-altogether unreceptive working class in the shape of moral motherhood and the family wage, as with other of the norms of urban domestic living.

The so-called middle class was by no means unitary; at the higher end were the owners of enterprises, whose family life tended to take on a dynastic character, as described for the Motte family of Roubaix in the north of France or in the memoirs of entrepreneurs like Schlumberger of Mulhouse in the east. At their great Sunday lunches the various branches of the extended family would gather together.[5] In the middle were the managers and the professionals, dependent upon income rather than upon capital. Below them was the petit bourgeoisie, the world of the small shopkeepers, traders and functionaries, which had again expanded with the growth of industrial consumer society in which workers had to purchase their daily needs as well as less urgent items on a totally different scale than heretofore.

The part that these various groups played over time changed with the Industrial Revolution, with an effective contraction of that of the aristocracy and landed gentry and a great expansion of the urban bourgeoisie in all its forms. But the shift in life-style and family life was greatest for the agricultural population as its way of life changed, more extensively in England than in France for example, with the virtual disappearance of the peasantry and their conversion first to workers under proto-industrialization with its domestic production, then at the end of the eighteenth century to factory hands under full industrialization.

Proto-industrialization

Proto-industrial activities in Europe have been recently discussed by historians as beginning in the sixteenth century. In fact such activities were present well beforehand, for example, in the production of pottery (red sigilata ware in southern Gaul in the second century CE which was exported to the north of Britain and to the south of India). Such productive processes profoundly affected the nature of family life of the participant, as did the more widespread work of artisans and merchants.

Let us concentrate on the later, preliminary, phases of the development of industrial production in Europe, especially in England, that ran from the sixteenth to the early nineteenth century.[6] These have been referred to as industrialization before the factory system and they were accompanied by the proletarianization of part of the rural work force. It was a form of enterprise that involved a close association between household production based on the family economy and the capitalist organization of trade, by way of putting-out and the marketing of products.[7] The producer was always directly or indirectly dependent on merchant capital.

The prerequisite for this development has been seen as the emergence of a body of under-employed rural workers combined with the demands of a world market for mass-produced handicrafts, a process that shifted production to the countryside.[8] These rural workers no longer had to take account of a balance between the available land and family size that is a feature of peasant households everywhere. Even with agriculture this constraint could in the end be over-ridden since 'surplus' children might migrate or open up new land; besides which there were always a number of landless or land-poor labourers in a village who had to sell their labour to those with direct access to land. With proto-industrial production, women and children all worked in the house, on weaving for example. The more children one had, the more labour was available for cottage industry, child labour being 'the capital of the poor man'. Hence among cottage workers fewer children went into service than in other rural households, marriage was earlier (there were no longer the same reasons for delay) and households were larger. The European marriage pattern had undergone far-reaching changes.

The role of women also changed. In the past some had always been employed 'productively' not only in running the house but in working on the farm. Sometimes indeed they took over entirely. If a farmer had no son to succeed him, it was customary for a widow or daughter to live on the holding and take over the entire responsibility for the farm. Other women were employed as dairymaids or as 'women servants in husbandry'.

Servants were usually hired at annual fairs or were pauper children who had been apprenticed to local farms, which in England were obliged to take them, but the practice largely disappeared in the course of the eighteenth century. This propensity to work outside the home has been regarded, somewhat unconvincingly, as a critical factor in the development of the workforce mobility needed for industrial capitalism, at least in comparison to China. One historian has recently claimed that it was neither technical inability nor population/resource imbalances but precisely the inability of women in China to work outside the home that prevented the widespread adoption of machinery requiring the extra-household use of female labour, that is, industrialization. In China they were prevented from doing so, it is suggested, by Confucian ethics, enforced by the state as a measure of social control. However, women certainly went to work in cotton mills in South China, encouraging their natal families to retain their labour even after marriage.

The rural situation changed rapidly at the time of proto-industrialization. In England in the early eighteenth century 30 per cent of land may have been in the hands of small landowners; a hundred years later it was down to 10 per cent. By the middle of the eighteenth century the majority of the population no longer worked on the land. Cities had grown with remarkable rapidity, but much surplus labour remained in the countryside. The same course of events occurred, more slowly, elsewhere in Europe. If there was less employment on the land, labour was available when 'homework' expanded.

In eighteenth-century Flanders it was the poorer areas that saw higher growth rates of rural industry and of population, which was linked to the lower age of first marriage and appears in the rise in the number of baptisms.[9] Those developments also saw a fall in real incomes.[10] Population growth emerges both as a cause and a consequence.

Sexuality

Some have also seen notions of sexuality changing in the new work situations of cottage industry. When people of both sexes work together, notes one commentator, 'they spend their time in idle intercourse which is commonly concerned with lust and lasciviousness, with fraud and theft'.[11] Both in England and France the age of sexual activity and of marriage dropped and the behaviour patterns of men and women became increasingly similar.[12] However, in the nineteenth century, both in England and France, the previous patterns of marriage persisted among children of craftsmen or peasants who had property to transmit.[13] The suggestions about changing sexuality under cottage industry run against the accounts of those historians who see the major shifts in sexual and family life as occurring only after the second half of the eighteenth century and as attributable to the 'market mentality' of emerging capitalism and the liberating effect of wage labour on women.[14]

Women's Labour

Regarding women's labour, in agricultural or other 'traditional' situations both husband and wife have always contributed to the economy of the household. What happened with proto-industrial activity was not altogether new, rather an expansion of an existing situation. If men had increasingly to engage in manufactures, so too did women and children; it required the whole family to support themselves economically. There was no full-time 'withdrawal' from participation (as later) either for housework or for schooling. That fact dominated the wages that people were paid, since they were remunerated on a family basis; it is a characteristic of the 'domestic (or, better, household) economy' that the family depends upon the labour or wages of all its members.

In the second half of the eighteenth century, the enclosures of common lands in England and elsewhere, the agricultural improvements and growth of population meant that with the disappearance of the joint resources and the establishment of larger, better-organized farms, a smaller percentage of rural people worked on their own plots. Many were employed by others; labouring men had difficulty in supporting the family alone, so women and children had to contribute through their labour, as they had always done on the farm beforehand.

The limited opportunities for men's agricultural labour ensured that both men and women had to seek and obtain employment in the craft or manufacturing sector but in work that could be carried out mainly in the home. Other women worked in field gangs or down the mines. At the same time the big farmers became richer but the cottagers and others who had partly depended on common lands were poorer. Even if there was still some labouring work for men, women ceased to be occupied in agricultural activity as they had been before; that was particularly hard for single mothers, but the contribution of married women to the family economy was also sorely needed, especially in the south of England, since men's wages were low and the price of bread rising well before the French wars. The new 'capitalist' farming provided little scope for employing women as day labourers, especially during the wars when a sixth of the pool of male labour was drafted into the forces. Their wages were half of those of a man's and they could undercut them on many jobs. But the war could not take up all the slack and rural rates of unemployment rose steeply in the early years of the nineteenth century when increasing numbers became destitute.

Before the Industrial Revolution, women worked at manufacture but were rarely given separate wages; in the eighteenth century their earnings were usually paid in consolidated form to the family. However many were not living in families; the high death rate left numerous widows, while the parish records give ample evidence of the number of deserted wives and unmarried mothers who had to support themselves or be supported by others.[15] Women's work was badly paid and oversupplied, especially in London where many unemployed girls had to turn to prostitution to earn a living.

When working for wages in the home they mostly took up those tasks in which they had already been partly engaged. Hand spinning, on which textile production depended, had long been the work of women and children. The yarn they produced was partly for domestic consumption but even in the indigenous states in northern Ghana, cotton was spun by women and the thread then sent to specialist male weavers for commercial as well as domestic purposes. With the expansion of trade in cloth in medieval Europe the spinning of wool became a critical constraint. The great demand for cloth meant a lot of work for female spinners; in the eighteenth century almost all the women and children in the populous counties of Norfolk and Suffolk were spinners but nevertheless

the yarn they produced was insufficient adequately to provide for
the Norwich weavers who had to supplement the local supply by
imports.[16] In that century 'almost every farm and most of the
cottages had a wheel or distaff as part of the ordinary household
furniture'. Some produced yarn from their own flax or wool, others
purchased for sale, but the majority were employed in putting-out,
working up materials owned by the employer for a wage. So the
proportion of capitalists grew, as did the rural proletariat. While
the rates of pay for this work were low in the seventeenth century,
they improved in the following one, at least until the introduction
of machinery after 1770, though rates were always variable.

Domestic Life

In what ways did this change in domestic production affect the
rural family? Obviously it gave a different dimension to parent–
child relations, since there was little space for 'the invention of
childhood' and the use of toys attributed to the middle classes
when children had to work so hard. They became even more valuable economically than in an agricultural context, which was one
reason for the increase in the size of families in the latter part of the
eighteenth century. Less was to be gained by restricting births when
there was nothing to divide among one's children, by endowment
or by inheritance.[17] And their value was apparent; in a sample of
budgets for the period 1790–1865, it was found that except in low-
wage agriculture the children's contribution to income exceeded
that of wives.[18]

The relation between husband and wife was necessarily more
functional than in the middle and upper classes; it was based on co-
operative or interlocking activities in the sphere of production. The
entire labour of the family was directed at the merchant and the
market; since it was no longer possible for most people to live off
a farm plot, they had to acquire cash (or goods) through the sale
of their products. A man's labour could not in itself bring in enough
income to support a family; it had to be supplemented by that of
wife and children, as it always had done in the agricultural sector
where the women's workload was often greater. Lone parents obviously had even more problems in coping. Only with the growth of
industrial production, with its greater profits, did it become
possible for some individuals (usually men) to earn a 'family wage',
that is, a wage for one individual sufficient to support a family.

Full Industrialization

The creation of factories in England around 1780 changed the situation of the rural proletariat still further by developing mechanization, which brought about the mass production of cotton textiles and the migration of workers to the new plants rather than the putting-out characteristic of the making of cloth under proto-industrial conditions.

Such reforms of production quickly spread to Europe and even more rapidly to New England, which imported not only the practices but the practitioners. It is from Europe overseas that I illustrate the way industrialization affected the family. The beginning of the Industrial Revolution in the United States is associated with the development of a cotton mill in Pawtucket, Rhode Island, in 1790. Pawtucket had been a centre of ship-building and therefore already had in place a number of the ancillary manufacturers needed to establish factory production, including expertise in the technology of water-power. Attempts had already been made to mechanize production, following the model established in England, but details of some of the processes were not fully known and above all the techniques of factory management, which could organize continuous production, were not available. That situation changed with the advent of Samuel Slater who had undergone a thorough apprenticeship in management in Derbyshire, England, but saw greater opportunities in the New World. There he was employed by a Quaker merchant from Providence, Moses Brown, and set about to create the additional machinery and introduce the complex system of factory production.

While the system was complex, the labour force to work it was not. Following English precedents, Slater employed children between 7 and 12 to operate the machines, not always the children of the poor. At the end of 1792, with his partners he constructed his own plant, Old Slater Mill, the first successful cotton mill built in America, perfecting the use of the Arkwright machinery of the 1760s. The Arkwright system followed on Hargreaves' invention of the spinning jenny between 1763 and 1768. He developed a spinning frame operated by the power of a large water wheel. The change had far-reaching implications. 'In his 1771 mill at Cromford, more yarn could be spun in one day than all the hand spinners in Rhode Island could spin in a year.'[19] Slater concentrated on producing simple materials in great quantity. At first progress was slow but in the twelve years after 1794, eighty-seven mills were built in the vicinity.

Indeed Moses Brown, who unlike his brother had refused to become involved in the slave trade, saw his mill as promising employment for both women and children who would otherwise have been deprived of work. Moreover the nimble fingers of small children were better for certain tasks such as tying broken thread. A 1641 decree of the General Court of Massachusetts Bay Colony had already propounded that children set to tend cattle should also 'bee set to some other impliment withal as spinning . . . knitting, weaving tape etc'.[20] The employment of this inexpensive labour in manufacturing enabled the early entrepreneurs to set up their factories and run them at a profit.

While many early workshops were extensions of domestic production, work in the mills differed from earlier labour for children either on the farm or in the house, where they were part of the family. In the mill, children worked away from home, on highly repetitive tasks, and were supervised by adults other than the parents. Subsequently whole families were recruited for the mill, often from neighbouring farms, providing a substantially higher income for rural inhabitants. In this way not only the children but whole families became involved. An advertisement of a fairly common type at the time from a local newspaper ran: 'Ten or twelve good respectable families consisting of four to five children each, from nine to sixteen years of age are wanted to work in a cotton mill in the vicinity of Providence.'[21] In this way industrial society developed. The employment of whole families led to mill villages being constructed, and some employers even set up schools for the children. Such schools preceded public provision by the state and were later taken over by church groups. But if children could earn they were rarely sent to school full-time; in 1796 Slater provided employees with Sunday instruction on the three R's. His efforts were not copied by all employers and there was often little pressure from the families to exclude children from work in order to allow them to take part in education as they said they could not live without the income they contributed. In 1881 the reformer Elizabeth Buffan Chace refers to 'this class in our population who learn to depend as easily on the labor of young boys and girls for bread as for rum and tobacco'.

The family system led to an increasing dependence on child labour and obviously encouraged fertility; the more children the greater the income, a situation that was to change radically with the development of full-time education. Meanwhile, children worked long hours and in very different conditions from their earlier rural environment. That contrast led to a movement by reformers for shorter hours and better conditions but the resistance of the employers was strong; Rhode Island textile industry did not accept a ten-hour day until 1885. It then came about because of the recognition of the need for education to encourage the 'deserving poor'. In 1882 towns were required to provide schools that were free to all and twelve years later a body of factory inspectors was created to monitor employment. But labour for those under 16 was not outlawed until as late as 1938.

Women's Labour

The coming of full industrialization has been seen as promoting the demand for the labour of women and children and encouraging high fertility. That high fertility was counteracted by the involvement of women and children in industrial labour which increased their mortality. Housing conditions were often poor, as Engels described. So bad were these in the first half of the nineteenth century that the death rates in cities averaged 20 to 25 per cent above those in the country.

In the eighteenth century women's manufacturing work was by no means limited to textiles and the smaller domestic industries; there were numerous crafts and trades in which they were engaged, either on their own account, or as married women working with their husbands. But except in trades conducted chiefly by women, 'the tendency was for women's activity in the business sphere to decrease during the period of the industrial revolution'.[22] This decrease is seen due partly to the reorganization demanded by economic changes, to the rise in wealth, to the separation of home from work, and to the increase in the capital required which meant that small producers no longer owned (or rented) the means of production. The influence of increased wealth had been noticeable from the later seventeenth century onwards, first among aristocratic women who took less interest in the running of their estates, then in the early eighteenth century the wife of an ambitious tradesman might aspire to a life of idleness in order to be considered a gentlewoman. 'They act as if they were ashamed of being tradesmen's wives', wrote Defoe.[23] Later with the coming of industrialization the notion was taken up by the better-off working class but also interpreted by reformers in terms of 'moral motherhood' and the greater obligations of a wife to children, home and husband.

Consequently the notion of the father as the unique breadwinner, which except among upper groups did not exist in the eighteenth century, was brought into prominence by the high wages paid for factory work, by the disappearance of much of the 'traditional' labour of women, by union agitation, and by Victorian sentiments about a wife's role that accompanied them. Many women were thereby elevated or relegated to the performance of domestic tasks alone, concentrating upon the bringing up of children including the supervision of their out-of-house, scholastic education which while it only became compulsory in the 1870s, was increasingly available to the working classes from the beginning of the century.

Full industrialization began with the cotton industry which expanded in the eighteenth century as the result of the increasing taste for Indian cottons described by Defoe and then the lowered cost of the manufactured product. While men were weavers of cotton, each weaver required from three to eight persons to prepare the yarn, a task that under domestic production might be done by his own family or perhaps outside but in any case it was undertaken by women, some of whom continued in this work even under industrial conditions.

The Factory and Handwork

The Industrial Revolution brought much of that home work in manufactures to an end, leading some women, mainly unmarried ones, to seek employment in the new factories. The majority of factory workers including women received higher wages than before, had better food and clothing, and enjoyed a higher standard of living.[24] The Industrial Revolution 'marked a real advance' in that men were now paid on a family basis, preparing the way 'for the more modern conception that in the rearing of children and in home-making, the married woman makes an adequate economic contribution'.[25] 'Modernity' in this instance did not last long. With this reorganization, however, many married women lost their economic independence, even the limited measure they had. But the single woman in industry was now better off, receiving her own wage as a matter of course and becoming more 'her own mistress'. The 'condition of woman' was generally raised, especially when the

Factory Acts had improved the working environment and excluded women from some of the more physically onerous occupations such as mining and foundries. Others laboured for low wages in domestic industries (especially in England)[26] or took up prostitution. But female factory workers looked down on both this kind of work and on a sheltered existence. It was mainly single women working in the factories; though they usually lived at home, they were paid as individuals, sometimes on rates comparable to men.[27] Certainly early Victorians would have wished to exclude them from factory work altogether and that did happen in some cases. But middle-class women were at the same time agitating for rights to independence, to education and training, and for admittance to industry and the professions. The domestic lives of this middle class, which provides the focus of most historical accounts of the family, was very different from that of the bulk of rural and urban labourers.

Machine spinning reduced the rates for handwork, though cheaper Irish imports also played a part. So too did the Napoleonic wars that raised the price of food at the same time as the enclosures had heightened the need of ordinary country dwellers for non-agricultural income. That reduction of rates was disastrous for many families who required the women's income to cover minimum costs. The first industry to be so affected was cotton by the lower rates for handwork. When machines were introduced, both men and women near the new factories were often paid higher wages than before. But on the new spinning machines women were increasingly displaced by men although in cotton there remained other opportunities for them, including weaving.[28] Those who suffered most were the inhabitants of the more distant villages where there existed no alternative to local handwork.

The woollen industry was longer established than cotton which was imported, and from the fourteenth century women had been employed in all branches and were enrolled as apprentices. As the industry became more organized women were again excluded from some branches because of competition with men. They mainly worked in carding and spinning, especially when their husbands were employed by clothiers outside the house. The extent of the weaving trade was enormous. It was claimed that 'there was probably not a town, village or hamlet throughout the . . . country which was not connected at some time or other with the manufacture of cloth'.[29] The result was that women's work had been in very great demand. That demand decreased with the increasing growth of clothiers' workshops and the adoption of new machinery; between 1795 and 1825 weaving gradually left the cottages until all such work disappeared altogether by 1850.

Poverty

The Industrial Revolution introduced radical changes in the domestic economy. The consolidated family wage disappeared and women virtually lost the capacity to earn in their own homes. So in rural areas the total family income was depleted; poor rates rose at the end of the eighteenth century, and it was some time before men's wages were adjusted to this change.

In England assistance for the unemployed was already implicit in the Old Poor Law. But apart from relief, the allowance system permitted the parish to top up low wages, with the result that some farmers would underpay their workers knowing the amount would be made up by the parish. This underpayment was one of the abuses the reforms of 1834 were designed to prevent.

The New Poor Law of 1834 in England abolished out-door relief and the allowance system; the only alternative was the workhouse itself. It had been anticipated that wages would rise now that allowances had gone and rates were lowered. That change did not happen at once. But a number of women and children took up employment to supplement the man's wage. The work they preferred was either domestic where the tasks were easier, or in factories where the pay was better. The wages for rural work were always low, because women's income was seen by employers as supplementing a man's earnings. So the employment of married women which helped to support the household served to keep down the wage rates of both men and women while the differential between them kept men out of jobs.[30] Low wages may have done the same for some women. The availability of poor relief seems to have meant a decline in the number of women involved in the knitting industry in the south which they were put off because of the remuneration.[31]

Mobility

Full industrialization required workers to move near the factories and to quit their previous habitat. Mobility was necessary for them to exploit new opportunities. They might make use of wider kinship ties in the initial movement to the town or factory centre, as has been shown for Lancashire (as well as for transatlantic migration).[32] Other working-class groups, as in Bethnal Green, used ties of kinship to create networks of support, but by and large bonds of neighbourhood were more significant. It has been argued that the small, elementary family is particularly adapted to capitalist activity, enabling people to move to seek work where it is to be found and to accumulate for themselves alone. While that may be true for the workers, for the entrepreneurs with their relatively fixed assets, with their ownership of the means of production and their desire to transmit their possessions to family members, whom they might use in employment or to raise capital, wider ties of kinship remained important. Much capitalist enterprise depended on family ties of the wider sort, from the Italian bankers in Tudor England to the boards of Sainsbury or Marks and Spencer. There is no indication, whatever sociologists may have claimed, that the extensive kin ties of Chinese, Indian or Japanese businessmen prevented them from engaging in capitalist activity, whether mercantile or industrial. Quite the contrary. The western notion, encapsulated in the idea that an anonymous multi-national bureaucracy would govern industrial activity (as a result of the 'management revolution'), has obscured a proper assessment of the role played by kin in much industrial and mercantile activity.

The Second Industrial Revolution

Industrialization and modernization are analytically distinct processes.[33] Following Rostow the first is often defined in terms of growth (the rise of real incomes per head), the latter in terms of rationality and maximization (self-interest). I have preferred to see the first as related to water- and steam-powered factory production and the second as a moving target of little analytical utility. What was the modern family for Pinchbeck or Stone no longer can be so considered; while Gidden's concept is all-embracing but vague and slippery. The development of industrialization in England was associated with the shortage of wood and the early dependence on coal (as a charcoal substitute), which was already exported in the medieval period. The mining of coal produced three-quarters of the registered patents between 1561 and 1668, eventually culminating in the development of water pumps and the steam-engine. Critical to this development were the invention not only of the steam-engine but of the coke-fired blast furnace and later the railway, all based on the growing iron industry together with the significant improvements in cotton production, which led to the factory system.

The situation for rural women then changed radically as a result of industrialization. While women's work on the farm had increased in the Agricultural Revolution of the eighteenth century by the second and third decades of the nineteenth they were employed mainly in the lighter agricultural tasks. That was partly due to the awakening of public conscience about women's strength, partly due to the protests of the women themselves, partly to the advent of agricultural machinery. There was also a greater demand for labour in the towns. By the end of the nineteenth century women had almost ceased to be employed as wage-earners in agriculture. Men's wages rose, especially after the forming of the Agricultural Labourers Union in the 1870s. That change was assisted by the development of machinery and by the shift from arable to pasture as the result of corn imports from the New World, leading to an increase in small holdings and dairying.

Working-class Communities

In the towns, to which many moved, the earlier disorganization of working-class districts in northern England has been vividly described by Engels. It was followed by the upgrading of housing, the re-establishment of more stable working-class communities, the increasing tendency to marry within the neighbourhood, and the dominance of female-centred institutions of domestic sharing among neighbours, well portrayed for London and related to the nature of work and to the predominance of mother-centred families.[34] In the words of one historian, 'private patriarchy' had almost disappeared from the urban working-class world: 'the husband was often made to feel like a bull-in-a-china shop, excluded from the emotional currents of the family . . . . The wife . . . was the one who maintained vital neighbourhood support, who negotiated with landlords and welfare workers, and who supervised the children's schooling.' The weekly budget was under her control and London magistrates sometimes spoke of the wife's 'headship of the home'.[35] That 'headship' also carried a major responsibility for feeding the family, possibly at the cost of depriving herself. Meanwhile the man, out at work in the daytime, found his companionship in the public house, a habit which could in turn lead to domestic violence. This tendency to matrifocality was apparent in nineteenth-century England when bilateral kin networks veered in that direction, with 66 per cent of widows living with daughters and 57 per cent of married children near the wife's kin.[36] That was also the case for widows in the early modern period.

Matrifocality

Studies of working-class relationships have stressed the continuing bond of mother and daughter in determining spatial proximity, allowing the mother's mother (in eastern Europe as in the West) to play a major part in looking after her grandchildren while the daughter is out working or even shopping. That relationship is psychologically strong because of the identification of the two female generations, especially after childbearing when both mothers will have gone through the same experiences and when the junior often depends upon the knowledge or support of the senior, and the senior on the companionship of the junior and her family. The closeness is of course much greater in every sense for a child than with the father's parents, who for the mother are in-laws rather than natal kin, a perception that is transferred to her daughter. The proximity has been emphasized in the studies on London's Bethnal Green and on Ship Street, Liverpool, while the prevalence of 'matrifocal families' has been shown not only in the Caribbean and among American Blacks but among 'lower-status' families in other regions of the world.[37] In some parts such closeness is reflected in the kinship terminology as when the term *nana* in southern England and *mémé* in France is reserved almost exclusively for the mother's mother rather than the paternal grandmother.[38] Does this not indicate a matriarchal rather than a patriarchal dimension?[39] Certainly the role of women as household managers and as increasingly independent agents in 'capitalist' societies should not be underplayed. Yet such a devaluation is what is being implied by the insistent use of the vague term 'patriarchy' to describe that system.

Marginal Men?

In matrifocal as distinct from traditional matrilineal structures (involving a clan organization, inheritance etc.), men are marginalized, whereas in the latter they are usually significant as 'mother's brothers'. That 'marginality' can often equal 'irresponsibility'. How far is this 'irresponsibility of fathers' a characteristic of modern industrial society more widely? Undoubtedly independent wage earning loosens the control of senior over junior generations as well as the economic relationship between husband and wife. No longer did marriage involve the transmission of 'productive' property. What devolved was less immediately critical to one's existence, and the dowry became transmuted into parental assistance in other ways (for education or for house-purchase).[40] That change involved a looser control of marriage and the earlier establishment of children as independent agents. Education for the children, which full-time motherhood certainly promoted, became general in Europe during the 1870s, with the next generation very much in view. This development, which put a virtual end to the entry of children into the labour market (learning was opposed to employment), meant that women as well as men were becoming better educated and later in the century were recruited to the new clerical work involved in running industry and the government bureaucracy as well as to school teaching and nursing, at least until they married. With their own incomes young men and women were able to set up on their own and make independent choices of a partner, who was no longer necessarily a life-long companion.[41] With increased mobility, a man might get a woman pregnant and then leave more easily for another job in another town (the quitting of jobs was more significant for ending employment than getting the sack, except in crises). That development was already remarked upon in the eighteenth century. 'Paternal desertion appears to have been a major factor in the rise of "illegitimate" childbirth . . . in six German villages in the first half of the eighteenth century, the couple eventually married in two-thirds of the first births conceived out of wedlock; a century later, just over half did.'[42] Is this the trend that continued in the phenomenon of 'dead-beat dads', of the male marginality in many working-class and Black communities at the present day? While there is certainly a great difference between failing to marry a pregnant lover and failing to support children after a longer relationship, the effects may be similar in terms of lone-parent families and their offspring.

Divorce

Freedom to choose a marriage partner implies freedom to end the union. The shift of jurisdiction over divorce in England in 1857 from ecclesiastical to lay courts initially affected only middle-class couples. The working class had long experienced separation and desertion but the Christian church had hitherto forbidden divorce and remarriage except in a very few circumstances. Inevitably the opportunities gradually widened to include the population at large, leading to the possibility of re-marriage as well as of cohabitation.

Consensual Unions

Extramarital liaisons, including those leading to the birth of children, are not the only aspect of the modern family and marriage that are prefigured in earlier working-class relationships. There was often an initial reluctance to enter into formal arrangements. Consensual unions had always been known but became much more common in the early nineteenth-century working class where they avoided expense and at the same time any permanent commitment. Church marriages were almost impossible to undo except for the very rich and powerful. But consensual unions could be dissolved by informal procedures, by 'wife sale' or by stepping backwards over the broomstick over which one had walked forward at marriage.[43] That changed in the twentieth century with much of the working class accepting the moral norms of the bourgeois family, at the same time as that family took on practices hitherto found only in lower groups. For example, apart from the self-acquired variety the dowry had disappeared, first among rural workers who accumulated their own and then among the proletariat who depended upon wages rather than capital. By the beginning of the twentieth century the dowry had virtually vanished even among the British middle classes, although persisting in France and southern Europe amongst the middle class until more recently.[44]

The Decline in Fertility

Women's labour disappeared from a number of industrial sectors such as mining, through pressure partly from the men who saw their wages as being held down, partly from outside reformers, partly from women themselves. It continued in a few areas such as those producing textiles, which experienced an earlier fertility decline among married women. With the Second Industrial Revolution the opportunities for women, many of them now educated, opened up. They worked in and gradually took over the clerical profession. From the 1880s more and more clerical work was being done by women – up to a quarter in some cities – and male clerks were led to protest at this 'slur on their manhood'.[45] They also dominated nursing and primary school teaching. And they made some major breaches into university education which made it possible for them to enter, at first in very small numbers, the 'liberal professions'.

Beginning in the last decade of the nineteenth century, fertility declined across the whole of northwest Europe (though it had begun to do so earlier in France). Between 1890 and 1920 it contracted by more than 10 per cent in over half the countries of Europe. While this was the period when contraceptive methods became more sophisticated and were adopted by upper- and middle-class couples, the working class only did so in the 1920s. Nevertheless the decline in their birthrates, even in consensual unions, had begun earlier as a result of 'natural' methods.[46]

The reduction of fertility obviously has some affinity with the growth of women's employment outside the home, as it does even more closely with the decline in child mortality – when that is high the fragility of life is likely to lead to over-compensation. However, the decline in fact began before the great rise in the numbers of 'working women'. That rise followed rather than pre-ceded, leading to the present situation where more women are employed in Britain (many part-time) than men, an extraordinary reversal in which Engels might have seen a disturbing dis-empowerment of men. While economic factors such as women's wage rates and the changing nature of 'work' are relevant, we must also see this development as linked to the education of women and to pressure from the women's movement as well as to considerations of equity, as for example embodied in the British Sex Disqualification (Removal) Act of 1919. But to revert to an earlier theme, whatever the demands made upon the family by capitalism there existed in the major Eurasian societies not merely so-called 'patriarchal' tendencies but also a long-standing hierarchical system in which it was important to maintain the status of daughters as well as of sons, not necessarily as equals but to distinguish them from the daughters of lower groups and to enable them to make marriages in the same or in a higher one (hypergamy). To insist on this long-standing feature is not to dwell upon the idea of an unchanging family but to recognize that such structural elements associated with the political economy may continue to play a role over time.[47] What I have called 'diverging devolution' adapts to new situations, providing at times a countervailing tendency that has its own logic of development as well as a measure of autonomy, promoted by the human agents whose interests are at stake.

Family Size

The earlier phase of high fertility passed with the coming of the Second Industrial Revolution that arose with the extensive use of steam power, especially in the railways. It began around 1873 with 'a swarm of technological breakthroughs and rapid product developments in steel, chemicals, electricity and gas motors'.[48] That was the period when Germany took over the earlier role of England as the leading industrial power in Europe, and the United states did so on the world scale. This shift is seen as resulting in a productive regime with 'an intensive mode of consuming labour-power, based on a reduced work-week, and a quieter, steadier pace of work under closer supervision'.[49] To that situation working-class couples responded by forging an intensive family economy where husbands increasingly became the breadwinners while their wives concentrated upon being full-time homemakers. The widespread adoption of 'moral motherhood' came when higher production meant higher wages which could serve as an adequate family wage.

Full industrialization, then, saw only a small proportion of the population employed in agriculture; even those who had to work for wages, whether on the land or elsewhere, were no longer concerned with the allocation of access to the means of production for their children. The population increased. But later on humanitarian movements, fear of competition and the desire for advancement excluded children from work and they were expected to attend full-time school. So their immediate value to the domestic economy diminished.

This was not the first time that the problem of family size had come to the fore; indeed I argue that in most peasant societies the actors make some calculation of the relation between people and resources. In urban Europe, Geneva is said to have started to control family size at the end of the seventeenth century. By the end of the eighteenth such control was common in France as it was in early nineteenth-century New England and in Holland where fertility was lower than in England; in the latter it only began its decline fifty years later. By the end of the nineteenth century, family size had dropped dramatically, even before the ready availability of contraceptive devices. This shift has been seen as arising from a culture of restraint, but if so that culture did not have an enduring life in the wider social sense except in so far as numbers of children were concerned.[50] Restraint is not a dominant characteristic of today's mass consumer cultures.

Fewer children meant a shorter period of childbearing for women, time to assist in the children's education or an opportunity to pursue at least a part-time career – and increasingly a full-time one. In this way women could become economically relatively independent of male partners. Some have seen this process of reduced fertility as leading to the modern family based on 'affective individualism' – a couple that have chosen freely to live together with their two children. If that can be considered a phase in the development of family structures it does not represent the end point, neither the present nor yet the future norms, which has taken a very different direction, as we see in the final chapter.

Europe Overseas

It is impossible to consider the family in Europe in the nineteenth century without taking account of the massive migration to overseas territories, which split existing households, distributed relatives around the world and led in effect to European patterns being established in other continents. That migration was made possible by colonial conquest, by population pressures at home and by opportunities abroad. All European nations exported part of their reserve armies of labour, concealing the imbalance between the growth of population and the opportunities for employment under industrialization. The movement was vast especially into those lands that had been sparsely populated by hunters and gatherers – much of America, Australasia and South Africa. There they were joined by Africans (forcibly imported through slavery), Indians, Japanese and Chinese, often as indentured labour. It was not a question of creating isolated family nuclei either in the Old or in the New World, since the dispersed migrants and the homelands continued actively to maintain a rich intercourse, as we see from studies such as those on the Polish peasant in America. Those continuing ties prepared the way for further step migration (especially family) for Europeans, who rapidly started a range of 'ethnic' associations, as well as for a returning tourism for the descendants of the migrants.

Earlier migrations of this kind had been stimulated by religious dissent, in an effort to break away from dominant creeds and find a haven where minority views might prevail. It was also largely agricultural, as in the case of much of the extensive migration that has always characterised the human species. But by the nineteenth century it became mainly secular and urban where the migrants entered the more anonymous world of the town in which there was space for privacy, for 'individualism' and for the avoidance or rejection of religious and other sanctions on interpersonal behaviour.

Local Migration

That was the case not only with migration abroad but with local movement to the towns, which reflected the pull of the cities (not always comprehensible under the conditions Engels and Orwell describe for northern England) as well as the push to get away from the ties and responsibilities (and support) of family living, a phenomenon that is only too familiar today.

Residence in the towns involved increased autonomy and privacy, more common in northern than southern Europe, where the climate encourages more public living outdoors. It is an aspect too of the dispersal of kin and of the isolated, family household. Privacy permitted the focusing on personal wishes, on freedom from restraint. It means that Catholics can ignore the ban on artificial contraception so that Italy can have one of the lowest birth rates in the world. At the same time the publicity surrounding abortion and divorce makes those particular prohibitions less easy to avoid. But privacy is not all freedom; it also entails less effective sanctions not only on unorthodox sex by consent but also on abuse of a variety of kinds, on women as well as on children. Abuse (a vague concept) has always been with us but it now appears to some to constitute a right rather than a deviancy; and if it remains deviant for the majority, becomes less easy to detect in the isolated nuclear household where 'affective individualism' reigns supreme.

Abuse

This important aspect of family life has received less than due attention from historians of past time and from anthropologists of present (but other) time. Like the extreme case of murder, abuse is largely a domestic phenomenon. One reason for its neglect has been that, like its quasi-opposite, sexuality, it is largely internal to the family, difficult to observe and absent from personal reports because both are seen as private and to some extent shameful.

Abuse takes two main forms, of women by men (mainly wives by husbands but occasionally sisters by brothers) and of children by adults (usually parents but also other kin and especially quasi-kin). Both sets of abusers held dominant roles in domestic groups. Not only social position was involved (and that did not normally countenance 'abuse', though it often permitted violence) but also physical strength that enabled rape for example to take place even when that was strictly forbidden by the norms and sanctions of family and society.

We are today very conscious of the amount of abuse suffered by women and children; it is said some 50 per cent of women have suffered at some time, though such calculations must always be subject to qualification since the criteria are rarely clear. Is abuse to be defined objectively or subjectively? Is every element of force, or the threat of force, even in sex, to be seen as abuse? Looking in overall terms not only at crime but at other forms of disapproved domestic violence, is this to be considered a constant in human society as the differentials in physical strength might suggest? Has it decreased with the so-called process of 'civilization'? Or has there on the contrary been an increase over time?

The evidence is hard to come by. A study of incestuous abuse in Germany from the seventeenth century analyses a number of cases that came before the courts, most frequently of step-fathers abusing step-daughters.[51] These cases usually became public because of subsequent childbirth – otherwise no 'harm' was said to be done. That fact alone makes it difficult to know if this level of abuse was simply the tip of an iceberg. But it could reasonably be held that in earlier times, when life was lived more openly between kin and neighbours and less in an enclosed box, that their watchful eyes kept a tighter reign on disapproved behaviour. Wife-beating may sometimes be accepted; the abuse of children rarely is. My own experience in Africa and India suggests that in face-to-face communities surveillance may well be more effective; there is a ready-made 'neighbourhood watch'. Certainly the levels of theft and of the unruliness of the young seem to be greater in contemporary society than in any previous one, though the violence of unmarried youths. especially among the nobility in medieval society, is well established.

Violence

Why should this be when in many respects present-day youth is so much better off, has been brought up in 'affective families' and belongs to a society that has undergone the 'modernization' and the 'civilization' of its manners and its emotions?[52] The paradox is plain to see. As many have pointed out, the decline in religious beliefs, sanctions and institutions that lies behind a number of the domestic 'freedoms' we are now enjoying, to marry closer kin (for example, cousins), to divorce spouses, not to support the old and indeed the young, also leads to a weakening of the sanctions on other interpersonal conduct.[53] That weakening is undoubtedly promoted by the market economy and is hence the other side of the coin to the supposed promotion of capitalism by the Protestant Ethic. But another factor threatening the structure of informal sanctions is the level of 'isolation' of the household from other kin and neighbours. Under this situation, abuse not only escapes attention but even when revealed may go unchecked, especially when it involves a household whose members are, for one reason or another, accomplices in the act.

The history of the family under proto-industrialization and the First and Second Industrial Revolutions shows a complex interaction between the economy and domestic life. Undoubtedly the most significant shift is that from mainly household production to industrial work in factory, office and shop. The move into towns led eventually to the establishment of some working-class communities, but these were always more precarious than in the village and in any case touched only a small proportion of the population

who otherwise lived in relatively anonymous and isolated circumstances. Under such conditions the informal frame of family life
could become much looser; for the majority ecclesiastical
constraints virtually disappeared. Women were increasingly
involved in paid work outside the home (after a period of withdrawal); for children it was quite the contrary, especially after the
1870s when they were made to attend compulsory school. After a
rise under proto-industrialization, fertility gradually fell as
domestic life began to face the further changes of the twentieth
century, especially those characterizing the Third Industrial
Revolution of the mid-twentieth century.

It is the proletarianization of the rural population and their fate
in the towns on which I have concentrated. But those same changes
in the economy led to the gradual marginalization of the aristocracy and the dominance of the bourgeoisie in all its forms. The
latter controlled the means of communication which disseminated
their ideas of family life to other classes, sometimes in the form of
creative literature, especially the novel and later the film. However,
those ideas were themselves being reshaped along some of the lines
which had marked working-class behaviour; the dowry disappeared, the choice of partner became freer, marriage became less
binding. At the same time some features of bourgeois conduct, not
so much of the dynasties of the factory owners but rather of their
managers, were adopted lower down; the decline in fertility, the
consumer culture (encouraged by and encouraging higher wages),
the investment in training. Indeed the educational system at the end
of the nineteenth century was one of the great factors encouraging
social mobility, doing away in part with the 'great divide' between
literate and illiterate cultures, stimulated by the gradual development of the mass media available to all in the extensive circulation
of newspapers, the publication of novels, the availability of the
cinema and the domestic penetration of the electronic media. As a
result there was a closing of part at least of the cultural and
economic differences between the classes, involving the expansion
of the middle class and the meritocracy, not only numerically but
also in terms of 'the ideal home' and what Henry Higgins referred
to disparagingly as 'middle-class morality'.[54] In all these ways the
gaps closed, though they were never eliminated.

One aspect of what we are dealing with here is the gradual shift
of work from the private to the public sphere. Under earlier conditions the work place and the household were identical for the
majority. But the transformation was slow. Even at the turn of this

century, for many girls it was acceptable to stay at home and work or not work; only at the bottom of the hierarchy did they work outside. In France in 1900 as many as one half, possibly two-thirds of the whole population, still worked at home. The numbers dropped off rapidly; by 1936 there were only some 351,000 home workers.

When girls went out to work, they often went into service in other people's home, a job with little privacy and little time for family life; children were unwelcome. Yet in France in 1892 there were still 1,800,000 servants in rural homes and in 1906 960,000 in bourgeois ones. For the latter family life was very different than for those they served, even though the situation was for them rarely permanent.[55]

In any case, this phenomenon practically disappeared in the course of the twentieth century, following the two world wars, and with it part at least of the class differences it sustained.

10
Modernization and the Family: The Theories

In these last two chapters I want to discuss the theories and the practice of the family in relation to such recent changes; I do so separately for the two seem to me to diverge significantly.

At all periods people have had theories about the family and the direction that change was or should be taking. Often these were ambivalent and even contradictory, as with Christ's well-known pronouncements in the New Testament. But this central focus in human life has always attracted thoughts, theories and proposals for change. We have seen how the tenets of Christianity changed domestic norms in the interests of the church and of God's supposed wishes. Much later the Reformation and Counter-Reformation had their own programmes.

The nineteenth century saw a vigorous movement directed to putting to right the wrongs seen as accruing from the development of industrial capitalism. Reformers of all hues played a part. Those interests also gave rise to wider reconsiderations of the place of women in society (and the beginnings of the modern women's movement), of the role of marriage, of the nature and history of the family, which was closely linked to the growth of anthropology and the comparative analysis of kinship, marriage and the family. A central figure in all these developments was Frederick Engels, who composed *The Origin of the Family* largely on the basis of Marx's notes on the book *Ancient Society* (1877), written by the American lawyer-anthropologist Lewis H. Morgan. Morgan perceived a gradual change over the very long-term from collective forms of marriage to the individualized monogamic institutions of contemporary Europe, thus setting the stage for a whole set of misunderstandings about the nature of the simpler societies and of subsequent history. Engels pushed the argument further, seeing the bourgeois family as inherently opposed to the re-collectivization of society under socialism, as denying equality of treatment to women and children, and as perpetuating inequality through inheritance.

Socialist Countries

Such propositions formed the basis of thinking and action about the family in the socialist governments that began to appear after the First World War and were extended with the defeat of Nazi Germany and its evacuation of eastern Europe in favour of the Soviet Union. Such regimes disappeared from 1989 onwards and now persist only outside Europe, in China, Cuba and marginally in South-East Asia, although in these areas too they have adapted to capitalist activity (just as in its turn the latter has adapted to socialistic, welfare, tendencies). Of course all such regimes have to raise capital for industrial enterprises but they tried to do so by collective, governmental means rather than privately through investors and entrepreneurs.

How did these regimes affect the family? They firmly set aside religious constraints and permitted divorce and abortion, lowering the birth rates, increasing the employment, education and the opportunities for women more generally, providing for the communal care of their children both in and out of school. In this sense there was less emphasis on the family, which, because the confiscatory taxes generated by the view that inheritance was responsible for inequalities (and in any case as with early Christianity that all property belonged to a higher authority), ceased to be important for the transmission of property and hence lost one of its main long-term functions in all other regimes. The effective confiscation at death of 'personal' property by the state seems to have diminished the incentive for individuals to save over the longer term at the same time as weakening the continuity of parent–child relationships.

The radical stance towards the family did not persist in its entirety. As women became better educated, their participation in the workforce grew and the number of children decreased. Familial interests persisted especially in agriculture despite collectivization; they persisted too in the education and subsequent careers of children. Particularly in wartime, the Soviet state was led to modify its policy towards the family which today in former Communist countries displays many of the features of other western societies.

The West: Sociological Theory

Let me turn to the discussions of the modern family by sociologists and historians coming from 'capitalist' countries. The family has long been seen by them as a critical feature of the processes that have variously been characterized as modernization, industrialization or the growth of capitalism. The two latter refer to the economy and are partly overlapping, with capitalism underlying both the mercantile and industrial aspects, and industrialization referring to a change that affected both capitalist and non-capitalist regimes alike. Modernization (and the cognate modernity) covers all these as well as the accompanying social changes in knowledge and in family systems. Modernization is a slippery concept. Literally, what is modern is always passing and how we choose to mark the beginning and the end (moving into post-modernism, for example) is quite arbitrary unless we offer some definition of its specific attributes. When that is done, this definition usually takes on a vague, ethnocentric, direction; this (modernity) is where *we* are now, this is where *you* others should be – if you want to develop as we have done in the past or as we are doing now.

The sociological discussions have seen modernization as the opposite of traditional (in the work of Weber for example), embodying individualistic as distinct from collective values, freedom as distinct from custom and constraint. Like many historians, they see these values as linked to the advent of the socio-economic changes associated with capitalism and industrialization, and that in turn with particular features of the western (or northwestern) European family. Most prominent in recent times has been the work of the American, Talcott Parsons, who saw the small nuclear family as being critical not only to the economic sphere but to modern life generally, since parents could invest sufficient energy and affect in their few children to enable them to take their place in the world while at the same time allowing the unit sufficient mobility to seek the best available work. The small nuclear family was considered to be functionally appropriate to capitalism, whereas 'traditional' societies were bound by wider and stronger kinship ties that inhibited independence and individuality and dispersed savings. It was argued that the 'nuclear family' or a small household is particularly adapted to industrial production, permitting the mobility of labour and employment under factory or indeed bureaucratic conditions. However, while industrialization tends to reduce the relevance of larger kin groups (for example, clans), it does not do away with all the wider ties of kinship. Nor is the nuclear family/household unique, nor absent from earlier social formations. It may be embedded in wider groupings but households in the sense of units of production and consumption are almost always of limited size.[1] What is different in the contemporary West is that the nuclear or elementary families are usually geographically separated ('isolated') from their kin, largely because of the demands of labour; jobs have to be taken where they exist.

The West: Historical Approaches

That notion was widely accepted. It fitted with Weber's attribution of the failure of the Chinese to develop capitalism to (among other things) the presence of wider kin groups. At the same time he saw a bureaucratic regime as necessary for modern society in which the eligibility of kin gives way to recruitment by examinations and other 'objective' tests. In fact at the level of the ownership of industry, and to some extent of its management, the family is still of great importance, partly because property continues to be transmitted between close kin. Regarding wider kin group, the theme was taken up by historians, particularly in demography by the work of the Cambridge Group. The latter reconstructed households from the numerous parish records at their disposal and found that as far back as the sixteenth century, England had had small households built around a nuclear family and that there was no evidence of ones with extended family occupation. As we have seen, this situation was held to be related to late marriage for both men and women, which enabled them to control the number of children, associated with high rates of celibacy and the practice of sending a proportion of adolescent children before marriage to work outside the home as 'life-cycle servants'. This European marriage pattern,

which was found by some to have emerged in England, characterized northwest Europe and gave it a family system which was what
capitalism needed, that is, small, isolated, nuclear families having
control of fertility and early work experience outside the home in
which the young could accumulate for an independent married life.
Late marriage, it was held, provided more experienced parents,
independent households, couples that constituted an 'affective
family'. So not only the direct economic worth of the 'nuclear
family' has been vaunted, but many historians, especially followers
of the *mentalités* approach, have seen the small family as encouraging close ties of affection between conjugal partners and
between parents and children; indeed the whole family is seen as
marked by affective individualism, in stark contrast it is claimed to
the domestic relations of earlier times and of other places. Like
Ariès, Stone places great emphasis on changes in child-rearing practices which he sees as creating among adults a sense of trust instead
of one of distrust.[2] As has been pointed out, even confining one's
attention to Europe, conjugal love was attested well before this
time, in Chaucer and Shakespeare as well as among the ancients.
Nor is there any convincing evidence for the radical changes in the
attitudes to children: even abandonment did not necessarily mean
lack of affection (any more than does abortion), or 'the lack of
warmth and tolerance in interpersonal relations' which has been
posited of earlier Britain and of such societies elsewhere.[3]
Differences there may well be but not at this level of generalized
mentalities.

The close ties between spouses is seen as linked to the freeing of
marriage choice from parental control and the substitution of 'love'
as the criterion for selection. The assertion that 'for those without
property, affective and companionate marital relations did not
develop before the nineteenth century' is not born out by studies of
other societies.[4] Was England or Europe so very peculiar in this
respect? That seems very doubtful.

While Stone discusses his idea that 'the great secular changes in
sexual attitudes and behaviour of the late seventeenth century and
eighteenth century cultures had nothing to do with the rise of capitalism', he presumably means by this industrial capitalism for he
does see them as related to the growth of the market and of mercantile activity. Another historian goes so far as to take the
view that 'Good mothering is an invention of modernization. In
traditional society, mothers viewed the development and happiness
of their infants younger than two with indifference'.[5] One reason

given for this unacceptable notion of both the modern and traditional was that so many of them died in infancy that they could
not afford to invest too much emotional capital. However, this
commentator sees high infant mortality as being the result rather
than the cause because of lack of maternal affection, a lack that
was only overcome by modern factory workers. All in all this view
is highly ethnocentric. That England and indeed Europe was hardly
a paradise for children in the nineteenth century can be seen from
the hard work and long hours that many were expected to accom-
plish. Among the silk weavers of Spitalfields children were
apprenticed to the loom in early childhood. In 1836 a Frenchman
was struck by their early age, the long hours and the conditions in
which they were expected to work – fourteen hours a day '*courbés
sur un métier*'. No wonder that one girl of eleven working for her
father was '*pâle et mélancholique*'.[6]

Indifference to Children

Some support for the indifference argument for earlier societies has
been found in the large-scale abandonment of legitimate children,
for example, in northern Italy.[7] However that may be, and alternative explanations involving the welfare of children have been
offered (many for example were reclaimed – it was often for the
parents a temporary foregoing), there is in my experience no
grounds for the notion of capitalism's invention of motherhood nor
of the indifference of mothers in traditional societies; I know of no
observers of African family life that have made such a suggestion.
Others have certainly linked the growth of abandonment with capitalism, and it seems to be the case that workers in early industry
sometimes found it difficult, not always through poverty, to look
after all their children and were in any case willing to exploit a
welfare loophole in pursuing their 'economy of expediency'.
Abandonment was in this limited sense an aspect of family planning. Regarding illegitimate children, poverty decreased the
chances that the father could or would marry the mother.

   In the early modern period, children were given pet names and
their loss was certainly mourned, despite the church's council about
stoicism in the face of God's will. Whatever wet-nursing went on,
it affected only some 4 per cent.[8] In any case it did not normally
indicate indifference to children; workers in the Lyons silk industry
sent their children away in order to protect them from the

dangerous working environment, as did many urban dwellers, though the mode of delivery of the children to the countryside could make life yet more dangerous since animal milk was not used for feeding to cover the period of transfer. Did the higher incidence of wet-nursing account for the fact that in England one in five noble boys died in infancy compared with an overall average of one in seven? The churches were against this (upper) practice and much popular sentiment was ambivalent; Rousseau advised mother's milk for others but sent his own children away. By mid-seventeenth century the Dutch middle classes had opted definitely for the mother's breast (perhaps they had long done so) but wet-nursing still continued elsewhere.

Probably children's health improved generally in the eighteenth century. Did attitudes towards them change as some have argued?[9] Were wet-nursing among the rich and child abandonment among the poor indications of the lack of emotional involvement? Some argue that children were wanted and looked after according to the standards of the day.[10] Child abandonment was largely concentrated in those cities that had established foundling hospitals: Italy from the fifteenth century, Paris in the seventeenth, London in the eighteenth. In nineteenth-century Italy some of these children were reclaimed, suggesting poverty as a cause for their temporary abandonment, but these institutions had been specifically set up to avoid infanticide attendant upon young mothers having to face the taint of an illegitimate birth, and thus enable them to get married.

Throughout Italy in the nineteenth century, some 90 per cent of illegitimate children from rural areas were abandoned because of external and internal pressures on the mothers. But in certain cities like Bologna and Milan, a high proportion of abandoned children from the town itself were the offspring of married couples (or mothers unable to feed them) who left their children at the foundling hospitals because of poverty; it was some of these who were later reclaimed. In the mid-nineteenth century a third of all legitimate children in Milan were left in this way; in Florence in the 1830s 43 per cent of all children baptized in the city were abandoned. Abandonment to charitable homes became a way of life, part of the economy of expediency for a large segment of the urban population, especially in the industrializing cities. The numbers began to drop only in the 1870s when the anonymous wheels in hospital walls, where children could be left without the recipients knowing the origin, began to be shut down.[11]

Between 1750 and 1850 there was a rise in illegitimacy rates throughout Europe. Why did so many women become pregnant without marrying and then often abandon their newborn? Some cases were due to the impediments placed in the way of marriage and to the difficulties of divorce until the middle of the nineteenth century. The first meant that informal unions ('fornication') could not be legitimized while the second had the same consequences for extra-marital affairs (adultery). Some writers attribute the rise of illegitimacy to a sexual liberation of women during this period, others to their greater victimization. Taking the first line some see the increase as due to the spread of market capitalism, encouraging the breakdown of family ties and the increasing freedom of young women.[12] But at the same time such women were less well protected by their families, or indeed by anyone else. It had long been the case that many women became pregnant before marriage but community pressures had led to the probability of a union subsequently taking place. This was no longer the case.

The 'Affective Family'?

An extensive historical treatment of the family in the early modern period has been undertaken by Laurence Stone who places the topic in the wider context of changes in mentality. That thesis is 'simply' stated by the author at the outset. 'It is an attempt to chart and document, to analyse and explain, some massive shifts in world views and value systems that occurred in England over a period of some three hundred years, from 1500 to 1800. The vast and elusive cultural changes expressed themselves in changes in the ways members of the family related to each other, in terms of legal arrangements, structure, custom, power, affect and sex'.[13] They were English changes and the critical one was that 'from distance, deference and patriarchy to . . . 'Affective Individualism', which he sees as the most important change in *mentalité* to have occurred in the early modern period, indeed possibly in the last thousand years of western history. These issues 'are central to the evolution of Western civilization'.

While the formulation seems to exaggerate the differences – earlier societies displayed both affection and individualism, later ones are marked by authority of parents over children – it is undoubtedly true that intergenerational relationships have been modified over the years. The senior generation no longer wields much authority in terms of marriage, nor of work or residence;

these latter are decided by the state (for schooling) and later by the individual as he or she obtains employment and leaves home. The timing of family fission varies in different parts of Europe, being in general earlier in the north where independence is promoted by state provision as well as by personal feelings and work opportunities. While both sons and daughters go off to set up on their own, or with partners, the elderly sometimes rejoin them as widows or widowers. More usually parents will come and live near one of their married children after retirement, not expecting financial aid but moral support and company, including that of their grandchildren.[14] This pattern is often marked by less tense relationships between the generations than in the past, when more was at stake; it is more distant in a physical and social sense, but closer in other ways.

These various approaches to the family that I have discussed tend to the idea of a 'modern family' of the cereal-packet variety, two loving parents, two loved children, marked by harmony and affection. Romantic love is a contributing feature, giving way in the eyes of a recent commentator to 'congruent love'.[15] Demographic trends are seen as moving inexorably towards the small, isolated, family of the kind that promotes the values these authors perceive in the contemporary world, the end point in a long and arduous evolution of domestic groups towards modernity.

'Love' and the Cereal Packet Family

This picture represents a highly idealized and schematic view which takes into account neither the complexities of the past nor the developments of the present. It is true that choices became more open for those wanting to get married; as dowry and endowment became of decreasing importance, so too did parental influence over relationships. But that had long been true of the propertyless classes and of those who had left home to act as life-cycle servants. And indeed of others too; the works of Chaucer and Dante, the plays of Shakespeare and the classical French dramatists, the poems of Donne and Petrarch, are replete with love relationships which take little account of parental wishes. But in the struggle between 'love' and 'duty', the former sometimes had to take a back seat, especially among the propertied classes.

Love did not always end up as marriage; there were high percentages of informal unions during the last two centuries, what we now refer to as cohabitation and see its presence as a sign of the changing times. It is not; neither is the dissolution of marriage, although in earlier Europe this was largely by death and sometimes by separation rather than by divorce. Death of course occurred much earlier, so that all unions lasted for shorter periods and left many young widows and fewer widowers in the population. Some of these remarried giving rise to complex families with step-children and step-parents comparable in some respects to those recently looked at in California.[16] These more complex units are in no sense features only of contemporary families as the stereotype of the 'wicked stepmother' in European folklore makes clear. And while divorce followed by remarriage was not possible under the earlier dispensation, separations did take place, principally as the result of men abandoning wives and failing to support children. Moreover violence and abuse were frequent but less publicized, more private, than today.

All this is far from the cereal-packet family, which existed as some idealized type. Unfortunately much of the analysis has been made in terms of just such general types as the affective family, in terms that is which do not sufficiently allow for counter-currents and conflicts, nor indeed for necessary temporal enchainments over time. Because families are necessarily linked in a chain over the generations, so that there has to be an overlapping or articulation of attitudes and behaviour rather than sudden revolutionary shifts. Except in marginal cases, we are dealing with changing variables over time rather than cataclysmic moves from one situation to the next. To talk of the end of the family, of marriage or of kinship, is to fall into this latter trap and to offer rhetoric rather than analysis. So let us turn to the practice rather than the theory of the modern family.

11

The Contemporary Family in Practice

The 'Working Wife' and the Structure of Employment

The second half of the nineteenth century saw the gradual spread of the disapproval of 'working wives', a sentiment which was earlier present among the aristocracy, was then taken up by the upper bourgeoisie at the beginning of the eighteenth century, and later by the upper elements of the working class.[1] Under the new circumstances of factory production, work, especially for a woman, meant something quite different than in previous times, since it involved long periods outside the house. Virtually for the first time, at least for the moral majority, the norm-setters, women's work conflicted with domestic roles. Disapproval of such work and its perceived incompatibily with the care of children and house was encapsulated in the ban on married women in the British Civil Service (though not in France) before the Second World War. It also led to stress being placed on the notion of 'moral motherhood', that caring for children and running a home was the most worthwhile, fulfilling role for wives. Such notions had been formulated earlier in the Industrial Revolution and already in the eighteenth century had affected members of the upper middle classes whose wives gained prestige by not 'working'. Now it was the turn of the upper working-class, although at a time when a counter-current was also developing.[2]

Let me insist that the notion of 'moral motherhood' should not lead us to think that earlier on mothers did not in fact care for their children. Some have seen the very concept of motherhood (like household) as having been born with capitalism while others have argued that the idea of childhood, of parental 'love', indeed of love itself, emerged at the Renaissance or with 'modernization'.[3] Such contentions have been rejected by medieval students,[4] and would certainly be denied by anthropologists and students of other cultures. It is true that for a while, except in the poorest groups, many married women did not participate in work outside the home, nor did much paid work within it. But that hiatus was directly related to the structure of employment, to the solidarity of male workers and with the Second Industrial Revolution to the aspirations of the petty-bourgeoisie and upper working-class concerning children's education (now compulsory) and better care and provision in improved housing.[5] The problems should be seen in these more concrete ways rather than in the highly generalized terms of maternal (or romantic) love and overall changes in mentalities of the kind elaborated in discussions of modernity.[6]

In early industrial societies many unmarried women had worked, in textiles, in service; with the Second Industrial Revolution, they began to fill many of the clerical jobs that the new industries and the state bureaucracy established. Eventually, with greater stress on women's secondary and higher education, with the support of women's movements, with the advent of mechanical aids in the home, with the need for money to acquire them and the rest of the increasing range of consumer goods, services and leisure, with the decreasing security of marriage, the 'working woman' became the norm. Today in northern Europe generally they form the majority of the workforce, if one includes part-time employment. In the 1950s between 10 and 15 per cent of married women were employed in Britain; by 1991 it was more than 50 per cent, nearly two thirds part-time. The Third Industrial Revolution of the post-Second World War has everywhere seen a radical change.[7] Since the late 1960s women in France have returned to the workforce in massive numbers, 44.6 per cent in 1986, a change that has affected family life in a variety of ways. A woman's birth calendar is often adjusted to suit her work schedule; her employment may be determined by proximity to the house and the flexibility of working hours. French women have always been employed on the labour market in greater numbers than other women in Europe, except for the former eastern block. In the USSR women gradually acquired a better education and they made up more than 50 per cent of the employment sector since the Second World War, whereas in 1922 the figure was only 25 per cent.[8]

As far as the family or household is concerned the most important aspect of industrialization was the dissolution of the domestic group as a unit of joint production with a largely common income, whether in agriculture (the farm family), as shopkeepers and artisans, or as proto-industrial workers attempting to survive on a mixture of gardening and out-work. Under those conditions the household income tended to be undifferentiated. Of course women, except for the poor, had access to dower as widows and before that could accumulate some 'pin or pig money' of their own, but as 'wives' they had no access to an independent income. With the increasing employment of women in their own right, they became potentially independent financially. They no longer had to remain in an unsatisfactory relationship. They could support themselves, at least with part-time work, which would later be supplemented with aid from the state.

Women's burgeoning employment has brought dramatic changes to family life. Childbearing and childcare conflict in obvious ways with work outside the home. As a result, few women today have more than two children, an increasing number only one, some none at all. That has been true throughout the continent. While the percentage of women in the workforce in the former USSR rose from a quarter in 1922 to half in recent times, the number of worker families with three or more children fell from 58 per cent to six per cent.[9] Even with this dramatic drop, problems arise with childcare because the provisions always appear inadequate, important as they are for a married woman with offspring to take a job. While men have shown some increased willingness to assist in the home, women in fact continue to provide the large bulk of the domestic services, such as cooking and the care of children and the house.

In these circumstances a woman's career is more likely to be interrupted and as a result she will receive lower wages over her lifetime, often not getting the same jobs because of breaks of continuity and even receiving less for the same work. The extent of the differential varies; in the USSR it was 30 per cent, but it is everywhere significant despite the thrust of compensatory legislation. A woman is also more likely to be out of work, on the principle 'last in, first out'. Given the recent high levels of unemployment, that constitutes a serious threat to the family income on which higher mortgages, longer holidays and all manner of additional consumption often depend. A married woman now works not only for her own satisfaction but to maintain a couple's standard of living in a society with high house prices and a level of comfort that requires expenditure on an increasing range of consumer goods whose production is itself essential to the economy and to continued employment.

Divorce

The percentage of women in work has risen coincidentally with the increase in divorce, with the number of single and lone parents, and with the proportion of unmarried couples. Whether there is a causal relationship is a matter of argument, but clearly access to a separate income promotes a woman's independence in her conjugal as in her natal family. The number of single mothers in the UK rose from 90,000 in 1971 to 430,000 twenty years later.[10] Among lone-parent families the rise in the divorced is almost as marked, from 120,000 to 420,000 over the same period. As I have stressed, divorce has only been possible for the majority since the church was made to give up its control over the establishment and dissolution of marriage, under the pressure of increasing secularization and state control as well as of feminist attempts to allow women to escape from intolerable situations as in the well-known case of the British reformer Caroline Norton in the nineteenth century. When the French Revolution made divorce possible in 1792, it was women who formed the majority of the applicants; in France in 1975 the parallel figure was 66 per cent.[11] The Napoleonic code of 1804 had made divorce more difficult and with the restoration of the monarchy in 1816 it again became impossible. Divorce was only reinstated in France in 1884 with custody of the children being awarded to the 'innocent spouse' (a concept now largely abandoned throughout the continent). Nevertheless it remained rare and remarriage continued to be stigmatized. From 1964 the rate rose significantly; divorce by mutual consent became possible in 1975 and the interests of the child were held to predominate in matters of custody. The stigmatization of remarriage was replaced by the stigmatization of solitude so that in some instances

the father tried to claim custody from the mother when he had
acquired a new wife.

In earlier times women's ability to survive divorce or splitting up
rested upon finding another partner, but with the possibility of an
independent income or of income support, from the former
partner, from their kin or from the state, those restrictions no
longer hold; lone parents can survive on their own, if meagrely.
Moreover, there is less call for them to get married in the first place;
single parents can maintain themselves by work, by calling upon
the father to contribute, or most importantly by seeking state aid.
This last provision now dominates all the other alternatives. A
woman no longer has to make a shotgun or informal marriage, to
hand her child over to some charity, or to depend on the largesse
of parents or of an ex-partner. State support supersedes other
forms, either by direct payments, or in France and some other
countries by making ample public provision for the care of young
children, at least after the age of three. While in France 93 per cent
of agriculturalists can keep their young children at home while
working on the farm (in the non-industrial sector), 81 per cent of
office and commercial employees have to find childcare outside the
home, with a relative (usually a grandmother), with a babyminder
or in a crèche. However, by the age of three almost all French children are at school.[12] Here as elsewhere single parenthood is made
possible to a significant extent by governmental forms of child
support; in the UK in 1990, 66 per cent of lone parents (i.e.,
including the divorced) depended entirely on state income support.
Of course this is true of the support of some other disadvantaged
categories: the unemployed, the old, the sick, the disabled. So that
assistance to these groups now takes up a major part of national
and local resources. For instance, in 1977 the Conseil Général of
the Lot in southwest France spent one third of its budget on 'action
sociale', with the French state itself being directly responsible for
the most expensive programmes.

State Support

In medieval times such aid was largely supplied by religious
foundations. These charities were 'nationalized' in Protestant
countries (as well as in Europe under the Napoleonic régime), being
replaced by some private charity but more importantly by relief
organized initially on a parish basis. That was the beginning of

renewed public intervention on behalf of individuals in need, which now forms a major part of the budgets of advanced nations. Not the beginning in absolute terms, since the Roman state had certainly intervened in domestic matters, providing bread and circuses for the towns, changing the laws on marriage and becoming involved in a number of other ways. But subsequently the Christian church had argued strongly against such interference, seeing family life as its own sphere of regulation. In modern Europe the state has increasingly resumed its earlier role.

The state primarily addresses individuals in need, for although families too are helped as they remain the unit of consumption, welfare funds, like wages, are increasingly made available to males or females separately. The changes in the economy and in support have produced a situation in which it is possible for an individual, even a woman with or without children, to live independently, although by so doing lone parents often put themselves well below the income bracket of those in partnerships.

This situation means that the allocation of property and money in divorce becomes of special importance. It is a remarkable fact that both in the UK and in the USA, as many as three-quarters of the absent parents (men in the vast majority) contribute nothing to the upkeep of their children by the parent with care, and the problem exists in most advanced countries. Throughout history in the West, women with children have often been abandoned. In earlier times kin would help out. One feature of the small nuclear family, separated from relatives, is that kin are less likely to assist since they get less reciprocal help themselves in their old age and in any case everybody 'values' their independence all around. They may provide some help but rarely in the regular way that abandonment requires. In principle, the father was always expected to make some provision, after separation as before. Even in the middle classes that is no longer true, let alone among the poorer strata. The state is left to pick up the tabs, for the public has in effect accepted the responsibility. The burden has increased enormously in the last ten years, making huge demands upon the large budgets already allocated to the social services.

The frequent dissolution of marriage and of partnerships obviously has a profound effect on interpersonal relationships between spouses, between former spouses and especially between children and parents. Let me first refer to property arrangements which are of fundamental importance. Frequent splitting up means that major shifts in property relations within the family (still the overwhelmingly predominant channel for transmission) occur not only at marriage and death but at a third point in the life-cycle, namely, at the dissolution of a union while the partners are living; the impermanency of marital unions may in turn affect the willingness of the parental generation to transfer property to the parties, which is in any case postponed through longevity, for fear it will fall into 'non-familial' hands. In the earlier period dissolution by death meant the surviving spouse usually remained in the house (or in some cases occupied a 'dower house') so there was no major problem in deciding on maintenance for her or for the children, nor yet in dividing the property between them. There was no 'splitting up', no radical rearrangement, involved. With divorce, on the other hand, every dissolution requires a settlement regarding support for the children, possibly maintenance for the wife (now drastically modified by women's increasing ability to do paid work), and the division of the couple's property.

These matters can be very contentious and costly, especially when the solutions are not standardized and involve the employment of lawyers and courts rather than direct access to moots and mediation. The ensuing disputes are destructive of social relationships and affect not only the spouses, who can separate, but over the longer term the children, who tend to suffer with split loyalties, and possibly in educational achievement, delinquency and in other ways. Housing (and more generally all 'real property') constitutes a particularly difficult problem since the dissolution of the union involves, for one person at least, a shift away from the household. That shift implies the provision of two lodgings instead of one, which may entail selling the original dwelling to buy two smaller units. If the new house of the parent with care is in a different neighbourhood, the move will disrupt schooling as well as the broader ties of friendship and of vicinity, of kith and kin. Complete disruption of this particular kind is rare since the parent with care (usually the woman) often retains the existing house. So the increase in divorced, together with the increase in single mothers, means greatly enlarging the housing stock and a significant reduction in the mean size of households.[13] In some major European cities one-person households are in the majority.

The problem of social relations between ex-spouses frequently centres around this division of property; later that turns on the division of time the children spend with their two parents.[14] The fact that less time is necessarily passed with fathers (usually the absent parent) contributes to their reluctance to provide support.

In that situation relationships become difficult, if they have not already done so, and love turns bitterly to hate. That change has a potent effect upon the children of the marriage, who directly experience the emotional aspects of the split between the couple; they may even be led to take sides with one party rather than the other, but nevertheless both parents continue to constitute their 'family'. Ties of marriage can be set aside, but not ties of filiation or even of parenthood (except in marginal cases). A tug-of-war is built into divorce, which inevitably affects the children of the union.

The situation is partially rectified by the establishment of step-parental relations. Such relationships are nothing new but they are more numerous and in earlier times they followed the sadness of death not the hate of divorce. Moreover in these 'reconstituted families' absent step-parents are inadequate substitutes for absent parents while residential ones are not only less stable but less likely to pay adequate attention if they start a second family. And the step-children are more open to abuse than own children.

Abuse

Child abuse is one of the problem areas of modern European society, in children's homes as in the family. It is difficult, if not impossible, to know if children were equally at risk in earlier times and in other cultures. But the openness with which sexuality is treated in the mass media, the extent of the commercialization of sex and pornography, are new factors which may lead to the promotion of alternative practices. With smaller households, with separation from kin, with the increase in step-parenthood, intra-family sanctions against 'incestuous' relations are less strong and the temptations greater. Certainly, splitting-up may produce stronger emotional ties in the children with the parent-in-care, with the absent parent however trying to make up by 'spoiling' the child in the limited time allotted to him or her (or else abandoning the attempt altogether).

An increasingly large number of children are affected in this way. In Britain in 1961 lone parents constituted 5.7 per cent of the families with children; twenty-six years later it was 14 per cent. Other European figures are similar whilst in the USA, often seen as the prospect before us, the figure in 1988 was 22.9 per cent.

One major problem is that the legal and normative systems are still basically constructed around a nuclear family dissolved only by death. The legal system is gradually adjusting to the increase in lone parents. For cohabitation, semi-contractual arrangements are being elaborated to take care of a split. With marriage the arrangements for dissolution are complicated and expensive, partly because many of the possessions of each partner have been merged together and so are difficult to disentangle. When it comes to separating, the principle of equality is held to apply but that does not always recognize the weaker position of the majority of wives in relation to employment, to pensions, to income, to financial and legal expertise, and simply in terms of bullying and *force majeure*. Divorce and separation settlements have a long way to go before they rectify this actual imbalance.

Ideologically the problem is that even today few enter into a union regarding it as being anything other than permanent. This assumption is not the case with Arab or Jewish marriages where the possibility of splitting up is built into the initial contract. But while such a split may eventually be recognized as a possibility by the partners, it is impossible to instil an acknowledgement of the potentially temporary nature of a marriage into the minds of children. For them the mother is always the mother and the father always the father. The roles are individualized, permanent and irreplaceable; hence the deep hurt experienced when a union is dissolved. Those wounds are something that society has to live with as best it can, as the reverse side of love marriages which can be dissolved when that sentiment no longer exists and a new loved one appears.

Secularization

I began with a discussion of the influence of the Christian church on Eurasian patterns of domestic life. Those particular influences have largely disappeared, except for some pockets such as Ireland where divorce and abortion are rejected. This situation has been brought about not only by changing ideological perspectives ('modernization'), nor by changing structures of employment (post-industrial capitalism) but by the parallel process of secularization.

An aspect of this process from the Renaissance onwards has been the general weakening of the religious control of domestic life, beginning with the Reformation. The schedule of prohibited marriages was relaxed under Protestantism; in the nineteenth century the ban on divorce was eroded, later that on adoption disappeared. These events happened in all European countries as the state took over substantial responsibility for laying down regulations touching upon domestic life. Gifts to the church gradually took forms other than major property transfers. A similar process of secularization occurred in Catholic milieux, where the state increasingly intervened. For example, what has been described as 'the second onslaught of Westernization' took place in the Spanish colonies in America as a result of the enlightened despotism of the Spanish Bourbons who reduced the privileges of the church, expelled the Jesuits (1767) and extended the influence of the state in family matters at the expense of ecclesiastical tribunals. With the coming of independence, civil weddings were established and more emphasis given to secular education, though the church usually continues to have its say.

Another aspect of secularization was the widespread use of contraceptives even by Catholics. However, the demographic decline which began to affect everybody towards the end of the nineteenth century did not await the advent of cheap and effective methods.[15] New means of contraception obviously made restriction easier, just as in the 1960s the pill played an important role in freeing female sexual behaviour and in what has been called the sexual revolution. But these methods were not intrinsic to the restriction on child-bearing (or to that revolution) that provided women with the freedom to do other things, to take part in activities outside the home and to devote more time to helping children at school. That change in fertility behaviour was an essential preliminary to the return of the working woman on a mass scale.

Of course restrictions on fertility had occurred earlier. Some demographers hold that western Europe had a special capacity for controlling population by varying the age at marriage. Such control (specifically by late marriage) is sometimes looked upon as a model for developing countries; it has been described as 'an in-built demographic regulation' that others lacked. But Europe is not the only area to have experienced moderate growth, nor is varying the age of marriage the only means of fertility control. Africa, which saw the birth of the human race, has long had a low population density; growth in China and India followed economic success. Indeed from many standpoints the population of industrialising countries in Europe ceased to be effectively controlled until the very end of the nineteenth century. Before that it experienced a dramatic rise in growth partly owing to the virtual end of the earlier need to match children with ongoing resources under proto and early industrial conditions where their labour had often become more immediately valuable. On the farm too their labour has been valuable but it had been accompanied by the concern to make provision for them to have access to the means of production or to alternative livelihoods. Later in the nineteenth century those ends had to be achieved through education, and concerns about numbers returned in a new guise.

Household Fission

Another feature that goes with smaller households and more lone parents is the greater reluctance of adult children to live with their parents or vice versa. It has long been true in western Europe that after marriage, a late marriage, the new couple established themselves on their own; many left home well before as in-living, life-cycle servants. But married couples often lived near their relatives and supported them in their old age, probably through a retirement contract whereby they took over the farm or other enterprise and the parents lived on a 'pension' they provided. While this contract might take a strict notarial form, the relationship was also marked by 'non-contractual' elements of a more affectionate or merely exchangist kind.

In Britain the junior generation still leaves home early, with those undergoing higher education supported until recently by residential grants. These awards are now less common but students may still prefer to take a loan against future income and gain earlier independence. In the rest of Europe, students are more likely to continue to study from home; in Italy even sons who are not studying tend to stay, while daughters too leave home only at a later age. But whenever they leave, there is nowadays a reluctance to return home later on in adversity – or to depend on parents for maintenance at any time. They would rather rely on the state whose support they take as a right. A right of course is relevant only if there is a corresponding duty on someone else's part, in this case the public's; all rights are 'human' but none are in-born or in-built – they are socially determined. While children do not continue to reside with parents, there is much evidence to show that in old age a significant proportion of the latter move to live near their offspring or other kin, and derive emotional and similar support from this situation. But as far as financial help goes, parents like children aim to establish their own funds which they are increasingly reluctant to pass on while living, although there are certainly continuing reciprocities between the generations. If the old have no such funds, they too rely on the state pension and on welfare services. In this broad sense, a culture of dependence has become widespread with the passing of extensive social legislation during the twentieth century. Its existence, however, is threatened by its very success since it involves a large and increasing proportion of the large and increasing public purse. That situation in itself contains the possibility of a potential reaction from those who have to contribute, resulting in pressures on political representatives to cut back the social budget and in the end perhaps forcing individuals to rely more on family and less on public welfare (as is still the case in Mediterranean Europe).

Lone Parents

The welfare backlash is often directed to single mothers although their presence is not new. In earlier Europe a significant number of women became pregnant before marriage; the unmarried state did not mean the rejection of sex or the adoption of a culture of restraint, as has been suggested – but on the other hand marriage or partnership was usually expected to follow pregnancy. The widespread custom of bundling or kiltgang involved the couple bedding down together over-night in the girl's house, even if full penetration should be avoided.[16] Avoidance did not invariably occur; hence the numbers of pre-marital pregnancies. Most such women got married, or on the continent abandoned their children to the care of foundling hospitals. As a result the number of single mothers was limited.

Today there are many more lone parents, through death but most commonly by divorce and through single motherhood. That trend is taking place not only throughout Europe but in most advanced countries. The alternative forms of 'family' involved are no longer deprecated as in earlier times but are accepted by the majority as normal ways of acting, as is increasingly the case with other forms of coupling, such as homosexuality and lesbianism. That constitutes a major transformation during the last twenty years.

The consequences are several. Firstly, more children are brought up by women, often alone, since in 90 per cent of cases they are the parents with care. As a result, fathers are marginalized in their first families and cannot provide much of a role model. Often enough they constitute the fallen idol, the God who failed. That failure must change the psychological patterns of family life. The father is 'killed' not by his successor, his son, but by his wife or by himself, in 'suicide' or resignation. The situation certainly produces a back-lash from fathers, sometimes directed to what they see as the triumph of feminism (or at least of women). As a result some take it out on the children, but whether or not they do so, it produces a crisis for them. Even if the evidence for their subsequent edu-cational attainment is ambiguous, the separation or non-existence of parents creates a problem for most that often continues after adolescence. They may find it less easy to adjust than do the separ-ating parents themselves who can more easily end affinity than children can modify kinship.

The process is linked to the existence of smaller households and smaller, more dispersed families. In both Paris and London the majority of dwellings are inhabited by one adult alone.[17] That diminution entails a great extension of housing needs. It also radically affects theories of the family under capitalism. Instead of the small isolated nuclear family, we get the yet smaller dispersed and fragmented family, indeed not a family at all if by that we refer to a couple living co-residentially with their children. The cereal-packet family turns out not to be an end point in modern-ization but a phase in family development which has moved on; a significant proportion, some 50 per cent, split up residentially and sentimentally leading to a period of lone parenthood for the participants, followed in many cases by remarriage and the for-mation of what have been called by some reconstituted (or 'post-modern') families and by others 'unclear families'.[18] 'Demariage' often leads to remarriage, to second liaisons which then take up the father's attention at the expense of the first and its children, but which are destined on average to last for less time than the original union.

The Conjugal Family

However, although there are more lone parents than before, this increase cannot be taken as signalling 'the end of the family', as is often claimed in popular journalism. For individuals escape from one relationship only to enter another. Of course, there are plenty of reasons why that should be: companionship, division of labour, some financial savings, sex, social expectations and entitlements. But the coupling does persist. A recent report of the London-based Family Policy Studies Centre concludes that despite continuing concern about change in the European Union, the evidence suggests that the family has retained its central place as a unit for socializing children.

So, in spite of these alternative arrangements, it remains true that most children in Europe grow up to adulthood with the parental couple. Those who do not often regret the fact and inevitably see the continuing nuclear family as the ideal since it keeps their mother and father together and in active if antagonistic communication. But an increasing proportion of the population experience life from a different angle. With the possibility of financial independence, with growing longevity so that a life-long marriage has doubled its duration since the nineteenth century, a lot is asked of a permanent commitment, especially when this is viewed as having to be based on love and free choice; when love fades, the obverse of the ideology is that you choose again and establish another relationship of what has been called 'congruent love'.[19] Such impermanence is the hidden implication of the romantic ideal.

This ideology spells the end of universal, permanent coupling (and therefore of universal, continuing, co-residential, nuclear families); a growing percentage of domestic groups become more complex as they become restructured. The majority of both divorced men and women marry other divorcees.[20] The resulting step-relationships, whether co-residential or not, become complicated in terms of the allocation of space, the allocation of money, and the allocation of time; the rituals of divided families are very spread out as are their holidays.

What I have tried to do in this essay is to indicate some major factors in the history of the family in Europe from the earliest times. I have aimed to avoid dwelling on the problem of that continent's uniqueness in the development of capitalism, industrialization or modernization. In terms of family, marriage and kinship Europe was unique in certain respects, as is every country, every unit. It is quite another question whether or not those 'unique' features have anything to do with the supposed socio-economic developments that gave birth to the 'European miracle' of capitalism, although in its earlier mercantile phases this 'miracle' was less unique than has been thought. That warning applies to the features of 'the European marriage pattern' proposed by the Cambridge Group and by other historical demographers, and even more to the less substantial claims of social historians concerning the 'mentalities' associated with the modern family (usually as a consequence rather than a cause). Those same doubts would also apply to other 'unique' features such as the bilateral inheritance of the German tribes and above all to the injunctions of the Christian Church. That organization took over much of the regulation of family life both from the community (some of whose earlier norms and interests had been very different and were now repressed by that church) and from the state. The latter intervened in family life in Rome, later made some incursions (for example, under the Reform and in nation states), but did not do so in a massive way until the process of secularization and laicization gained the upper hand in the nineteenth century, with the coming of industrial capitalism.

There is, in my view, little evidence that the European family facilitated capitalism. If we are referring to mercantile capitalism and to the entrepreneurship required for proto-industrial production, distribution and trade, then these developments were in no way limited to the West. They were found with silk, porcelain and bronzes in China, with cottons in India, with pottery in the earlier Mediterranean. The respective family systems were very varied. However, if we are referring to industrial capitalism, then its development at the end of the eighteenth century was certainly centred on western Europe, but there seems to have been little in this particular change for the family to inhibit or to aid. Family structures have not prevented industrialization in Osaka, in Ahmadabad or in Shanghai, although the particular form that process takes may have been influenced by its nature, its finances and its wider relationships.

Modernization is the third description (after capitalism and industrialization) of what needs to be explained but it is clearly a moving target, hence the need to bring in concepts like postmodernism. I have insisted that dichotomies like 'modern' and 'traditional', beloved by sociologists and historians alike, are useful only as vague signposts, not as analytic tools. There is no agreement on what constitutes modern (or modernity), hence no agreement on what needs to be explained. In family studies one writer chooses one set of positive features, such as the affective family; another a set of negative ones, such as frequent divorce.

Family life certainly changed after the Renaissance and the Reformation, though for the majority not in the dramatic way that has been seen by some. The advent of Protestantism (following earlier 'heresies'), the modification of Catholic norms, and the gradual process of secularization, initiated changes in whom one could marry. That subject was of great importance in rural society where it affected the transmission of land and property, leading in Catholic regions to insistent requests for indulgences and dispensations of which Luther so strongly disapproved. Prohibitions were important too in towns as we see from the extensive writings about the prohibited degrees, in particular about marriage to the dead wife's sister, that appeared in Britain in the nineteenth century and that set the stage for the scholarly interest in the 'universality' of the incest 'taboo' towards the end of that period. But above all family life changed with the Industrial Revolution, as observers like Engels noted, with the great shifts in the ways in which men, women and children were able to gain a livelihood. For the majority the close dependence of family life on the domestic economy was loosened. The political system, the pressure of interest groups, the freedoms and opportunities of a financial and educational kind, together with others generated by the mass media, played a greater part. But these developments were not random, nor altogether voluntaristic. For parallel changes took place throughout the major part of Europe, with some significant internal variations between north and south, east and west, Protestant and Catholic. Industrialization has tended to reduce those differences within Europe and other advanced countries and to produce similar trajectories in the development of domestic life across the whole continent. The process continued with the Second Industrial Revolution that in Europe centred on Germany and introduced greater opportunities for women than under 'smoke-stack' industries, in clerical, distributive and teaching work. The spread of education opened the way to the yet more extensive possibilities under the Third Industrial Revolution of post-war Europe and America, with its concentration on lighter industry and on the service and media sectors. Stimulated by the women's movement and by liberal ideologies more generally, such changes had significant effects on power and tasks within the domestic group as well as on the sexual revolution of the 1960s. Both the expenses of consumption and the productive system of consumer society demanded the participation of 'working wives' and of working women as a whole. In this way the economy and secular ideologies have gradually taken over as the major factors from the interests of the church and of religious organizations, modifying the contours of family life.

Notes

Preface

1 Especially Saller (1991), Treggiari (1991) and Corbier (1991).
2 On the early medieval period I have used in particular Murray (1983) and Wemple (1981) and on the later the work of Herlihy (1985) and Razi (1980). For the early modern period I have always had help from members of the Cambridge Group, especially Laslett, Wrigley, Smith and Wrightson as well as my colleague Macfarlane. For the seventeeth and eighteenth centuries I have used Stone but have depended above all on Hufton (1995). For the nineteenth century I have used a variety of sources, old ones such as Engels and Pinchbeck (1930), whose work has been criticised but mostly supported by Humphries, as well as more recent works by Segalen (1981), Shorter (1975), Seccombe (1991, 1993), and others; for the contemporary family I have used the sources incorporated in the joint work referred to above.

1   The Beginnings

1 Goody (1990).
2 Saller (1991).
3 Shaw (1991): 72
4 Klapisch-Zuber (1985).

5   Couroucli (1985).
6   As W. H. R. Rivers pointed out many years ago.
7   As Stone (1977), Ariès (1962) and Shorter (1975) respectively
    suggest.
8   That is a theme to which I shall return in chapter 8.
9   Goody (1990), ch. 16
10 For example, in the writings of Trevor-Roper.
11 J. Goody a raison. Cette collection a pris comme définition de
    l'Europe celle sur laquelle discutent – car elle est problématique –
    historiens et politiques aujourd'hui. Elle tient largement compte de
    la diversité des composantes et de l'évolution historique évoquées ici
    par J. Goody qui s'attaque à des idées reçues.' – J. Le G.
12 Goody (1976)
13 Medick (1976): 303 on protoindustrialization
14 Pinchbeck (1969): 179
15 Medick (1976): 312 quoting Wittfogel.
16 Kertzer and Saller (1991).
17 Guichard and Cuvillier (1996) [1986].
18 For Gypsies, see Okely (1983) and Stewart (1997). For the Jews, see
    Zbarowski and Herzog (1952).
19 Guichard (1977).
20 Goody (1983).
21 Shorter (1975).
22 Stone (1977).
23 See the debate between Stone (1986) and Macfarlane (1986).
24 Macfarlane (1978).

2   The Heritage of Greece and Rome

1   For further information about Greece, see Finley (1955), Lacey
    (1968) and the discussion and references in Goody (1990).
2   Treggiari (1991): 466.
3   For example G. D. Thompson (1949), who follows Engels.
4   See for example Goody (1983), and for a broader discussion (1990).
5   Saller (1991): 24.
6   Treggiari (1991): 466–7.
7   Guichard and Cuvillier (1996): 326.
8   Guichard and Cuvillier (1986): 327.
9   Pomata (1996): 59.
10 Pomata (1996): 59.
11 Klapisch-Zuber (1996): 110.
12 Shaw (1991).
13 Garnsey (1991).
14 Ariès (1962): 37.

15 Shaw (1991).
16 By Vovelle.
17 Shaw (1991): 89–90.
18 Treggiari (1991): 105.
19 Saller (1991): 380.
20 Kertzer and Saller (1991): 10.
21 Sabean points out that both he for Germany and Delille for Italy have shown that the prohibition on close marriage collapsed all over Europe in the nineteenth century among the property holding classes and that after the First World War cousin marriages declined in importance. While the practice declined, the objections to cousin marriage remained until recently in Catholic as well as in some Protestant dogma. On the other hand practice always varied, close marriage being important as long as property transfer at marriage was significant. But with the decline of the dowry and of the importance of devolution more generally, the attraction of such marriages disappeared.
22 Corbier (1991): 140; Shaw and Saller (1984); Goody (1983). For example, Corbier declares that we should eliminate the Calpurnii Pisones from the list of family trees used by Shaw and Saller to demonstrate the absence of marriage between cousins within a legally recognized degree (Corbier 1991: 141 where she gives other examples).
23 Corbier (1991): 140.
24 Goody (1983): 31. I never considered the Roman system as endogamous (Corbier 1991: 134), only that certain marriages were 'close'.
25 Corbier (1991).
26 Goody (1983): 31.
27 Corbier (1991). Sabean (personal communication) remarks that there is considerable growing evidence that from the late middle ages to the late eighteenth century there was a structurally specific area of kinship where people did not marry endogamously as far as class was concerned, although endogamy was more prevalent in the nineteenth century. While variations occurred, by and large land sought land, wealth wealth and upbringing upbringing.
28 Treggiari (1991): 103.
29 Shaw and Saller (1984); Treggiari (1991): 103.
30 Treggiari (1991): 106. See Veyne (1978).
31 Saller (1991): 24.
32 Sheehan (1991): 72.
33 Corbier (1991): 128.
34 Corbier (1991): 44.
35 Goody (1983).

3 The Coming of Christianity

1 Veyne (1978) and Wempel (1981) respectively.
2 Dumont (1981) and Macfarlane (1978) respectively.
3 Sheehan (1991): 179.
4 See Goody (1990). The one exception was North India where marriages were forbidden within the patrilineage, though marriages to very close kin flourished in South India.
5 Goody (1990), ch. 10.
6 Klapisch-Zuber (1996): 109–10.
7 Ferrante (1996): 115.
8 Ferrante (1996): 126.
9 MacCormack (1997): 669.
10 Rawson (1991).
11 Saller (1991): 342.
12 Sheehan (1991): 177.
13 MacCormack (1997): 661.
14 On the early history of godparenthood, arising out of baptismal sponsorship already present in Augustine's day, see MacCormack (1997): 655, Lynch (1986). Such kin were explicitly excluded from marriage in a law of Justinian dated 830 CE.
15 MacCormack (1997): 670.
16 Wemple (1981): 149.
17 Bremmer and van den Bosch (1994): 49–50.
18 Bremmer and van den Bosch (1994): 42.
19 Bremmer and van den Bosch (1994): 43.
20 Bremmer and van den Bosch (1994): 47.
21 Jerome, *Ep.* 127.3.
22 J. Bremmer (1994): 48.
23 J. Bremmer (1994): 48–9.
24 according to Speiser.
25 Sheehan (1991): 181.
26 MacCormack (1997): 653.
27 MacCormack (1997): 654.
28 Hodges (1982): 121.
29 J. Bremmer (1994): 43, following the argument of P. Brown.
30 Hufton (1995): 62.
31 Saller (1991).
32 Kertzer (1993).
33 Saller (1991): 340.
34 Bernand and Gruzinski (1996): 172.
35 Bernand and Gruzinski (1996): 173.
36 Bernand and Gruzinski (1996): 173.

4   The German Lands

1   Summarized in Guichard and Cuvillier (1996).
2   G. D. Thompson (1949); Wemple (1981): 10.
3   Phillpots (1913).
4   Murray (1983).
5   Guichard and Cuvillier (1996): 345.
6   Guichard and Cuvillier (1996): 345.
7   Wemple (1981): 2.
8   Wemple (1981): 2.
9   Wemple (1981).
10 King (1972): 223.
11 Phillpots 1931: 254.
12 Wickham (1994): 257.
13 Engels (1972): 215.
14 Wickham (1994): 259.
15 Wemple (1981): 107, after Herlihy.
16 Wickham (1994): 248, 255.
17 Wolf (1966).
18 Seccombe (1991).
19 On France for the sixteenth century (but doubtless earlier) see Yver (1966). On England see Homans (1941).
20 Wemple (1981): 2.
21 Wemple (1981): 76.
22 Wemple (1981): 36.
23 Wemple (1981): 70.
24 Wemple (1981): 43.
25 Wemple (1981): 83–4.
26 Wemple (1981): 87.
27 Wemple (1981): 31.
28 Gies (1987).
29 Wemple (1981): 122.
30 Wemple (1981) sees the difference in women donors and co-donors as fluctuating between about 28 per cent in the early period and 19.6 per cent in the later one.
31 Wemple (1981): 122.
32 Goody (1990).
33 Wemple (1981): 57.
34 Wemple (1981): 89.
35 Sabean (personal communication) sees this as especially important in the nineteenth century
36 Bede, *Historia Ecclesiastica*, Bk. II, ch 5.
37 According to Ermoldus Nigellus, 'Carmen in Loisorem Hludowici 3'; Wemple (1981): 116, 123.

38 E. P. Thompson (1991); Menefee (1981).
39 Sole (1976).
40 According to Sabean (personal communication) its appearance correlated with formal catechism instruction but there has been a general view that the German tradition was marked by freer forms of marriage than the Roman or Christian; it is by no means clear that one can make such a distinction
41 Herlihy (1985).

5   European Patterns and Medieval Regimes

1   Duby (1978).
2   Yver (1966).
3   Razi (1980).
4   Seccombe (1991).
5   Goody (1990); Gaunt (1983).
6   Sabean (1990).
7   Such a procedure has possible dangers but is analytically profitable.
8   Hajnal (1982): 469, 482.
9   Sabean (1990): 266 The Hungarian figures refer to the total population while the Neckarhausen pertain to the village.
10 Sabean (1990): 267. For an earlier example from England see Razi (1980) on Halesowen in the fourteenth century.
11 Wrightson (1981): 152–3 discussing the work of Chaytor (1980).
12 Laslett (1972): 27.
13 Chaytor (1980).
14 Wrightson (1981), who drew my attention to Tadmor (1996).
15 For Corfu see Couroucli (1985); for Florence see Klapisch-Zuber (1985, 1991). In the Scottish Border country 'surnames' indicating patronymic kin groups (Armstrongs, Grahams) seem to have emerged under feuding conditions after 1300 until the pacification of the late sixteenth century (Wrightson, personal communication)
16 Klapisch-Zuber (1991): 228.
17 Ariès (1962).
18 Shahar (1990).
19 Stone (1977).
20 Macfarlane (1978); Laslett (1976).
21 See Herlihy (1985).
22 Laslett (1972).
23 Hajnal (1982): 464.
24 Hajnal (1982): 476.
25 R. M. Smith (1979).
26 See Seccombe's acceptance of this suggestion (1991), even though he is critical of other aspects of the discussion.

27   Chaytor (1980): 27, 28.
28   Chaytor (1980): 60.
29   Chaytor (1980): 27 The reference is to Laslett's article on 'Familie und Industrialisierung'.
30   Wickham (1994): 267 Land transfers seem to have been predominantly within the family until the fifteenth century when its greater availability is associated with extra-familial transactions, at least to the end of that century. A recent study of Norfolk shows that in the early sixteenth century when land is again getting scarcer, the trend is reversed (Wrightson, personal communication, referring to the research of Jane Whittle).
31   Sheehan (1991).
32   Kertzer and Saller (1991): 148.

6   Women, Children and Fathers in the Reformation and Counter-Reformation

1   See the works by Herlihy and Klapisch-Zuber (1978), by Nicholas (1985) and by Homans (1941) respectively.
2   This suggestion comes from J Mitchell.
3   McCabe (1993): 55.
4   McCabe (1993): 292.
5   Ravis-Giordani (1994): 11.
6   Hufton (1995): 392.
7   J. Le Goff, Preface to Greilsammer (1990), quoting Pedro Cornejo.
8   Maynes (1996): 266.
9   Stone (1977).
10   Ingram (1987): 5.
11   Ingram (1987): 11.
12   Ferrante (1996).
13   Hufton (1995): 259.
14   Hufton (1995): 260.
15   Hufton (1995): 221.
16   For the Wyf of Bath, see Chaucer, The Canterbury Tales: for the Paston letters, see the work of Bennett. For a later period see Davis (1995) and Ozouf (1995).
17   Religion affected death in other ways; in the south there were more elaborate rituals for celebrating the dead, whereas in the north doubts about expenditure on funerals were more in evidence; as with remarriage this difference was encouraged by the Protestant–Catholic split
18   Hufton (1995): 245.
19   Hufton (1995): 320.
20   Kertzer (1993): 57.

21 Boswell (1988); Kertzer (1993): 9.
22 Kertzer (1993): 24.
23 Stone (1992).
24 Martin and Lefaucheur (1995): 10.
25 Kertzer (1993): 78; in 1875 91 per cent of all illegitimate children were abandoned.
26 Martin and Lefaucheur (1995): 18.
27 Martin and Lefaucheur (1995): 16.
28 Laslett (1977).
29 Pinchbeck (1930): 75 and 76.
30 Hufton (1995): 332.
31 There were not a great number of dispensations in France for a century after the Council of Trent. Those that were granted might be challenged in the civil courts, leading to grave splits in powerful families in the seventeenth century.
32 Delumeau in *Sin and Fear* (1990) has argued that there was a tightening up of ecclesiastical control in Catholic countries in the sixteenth and seventeenth centuries (associated with the Counter-Reformation) and an easing in the eighteenth century, perhaps due more to mobility than to the Enlightenment (Hufton, personal communication).
33 Kertzer (1993): 23.
34 Hufton (1995): 357.
35 Hufton (1995): 288.
36 Hufton (1995).
37 On industrialization and the family see Segalen (1996): ii, 377ff and Seccombe (1993).

7   Dowry and the Rights of Women

1 Goody (1976).
2 Brettel (1991).
3 The literature on dowry in Europe has grown vigorously in the last years, stimulated by the interest in women and women's history generated by Second-wave Feminism. It would take a book in itself to discuss this material, which I have had to treat in a very general way. But one comment is called for. There is a tendency in some feminist writing to see women as victims because they did not inherit. That is to neglect the fact that both dowry and inheritance are aspects of devolution and younger sons too might be endowed at marriage in a way that excluded them from subsequent partition, giving the mistaken appearance of an absolute primogeniture.
4 Goody (1962) and (1966).
5 Hanawalt (1996): 202; (1986).

6   For example, in Finland but the same holds for south-west France (JRG fieldnotes).
7   Ferrante (1996): 115.
8   Mundy (1991): 150.
9   Kirshner (1991): 194.
10 Hufton (1998).
11 Haynes in Maynes (1996).
12 Hufton (1995): 91. The British and Dutch working classes in towns seem the first to abandon dowry which could then take the residual form of a bottom draw of textiles (Hufton, personal communication).
13 For Greece see references in Goody (1990): ch. 15; for Italy see J Davis (1973).
14 Hufton (1995): 91.
15 Goody (1990).
16 Hufton (1995): 291.
17 B. Hill (1989). Hills' figures are disputed: Laslett suggests that if continuing unions in a community are at issue, particularly those with resident children, the figure must have been well below 10 per cent, but if it is a matter of unions originally contracted outside the church, that is, including non-conformist and clandestine marriages, the figure could be 20 per cent or higher (Laslett, personal communication).
18 Hufton (1995).
19 Goody (1990): ch. 15.
20 Hufton (1995): 254.
21 Other middle-class women (Amazons) saw military service as linked to citizenship and wanted to participate for this reason but this proposal gained little support as most women did not want to fight for their country.
22 Goody (1990): ch. 7; Hufton (1995): 67.
23 Hufton (1995): 252.
24 Saller 1988: 408–9 quoted in Kirshner (1991): 190.
25 Galt (1991): 308.
26 Davis (1973).
27 Galt (1991).
28 Galt (1991): 317; also Brettel (1991): 342 for Greece.
29 Kirshner (1991): 200; Davis (1973); Brettel (1991).
30 Loizos (1975).
31 Seccombe (1991): 65.
32 Seccombe (1991): 277.
33 Seccombe (1991).

8   The Differences

1   See Guichard (1977).
2   Hufton (1995): 140. See above, p. 92.
3   Hufton (1995).
4   Hufton (1995): 258.
5   Peristiany and Pitt-Rivers (eds) (1991).
6   Banfield (1958).
7   Hufton (1995): 100.
8   Yver (1966).
9   Jones (1985): 103.
10 Edward Barker, quoted Jones (1985): 104.
11 Ingram (1987): 18.
12 Czap (1982a), (1982b).
13 Hajnal (1982): 468.
14 Herlihy and Klapisch-Zuber (1978).
15 Barbagli (1991); Rowland (1986).
16 Barbagli (1991) See also the splendid film of McDougall on Sardinian shepherds.
17 Quoted Barbagli (1991): 268.
18 Barbagli (1991).
19 Todorova (1993): 126; Hammel (1972).
20 Todorova (1993): 170.
21 Czap (1982a) and (1982b).
22 Todorova (1993): 33.
23 Goody (1990): ch. 12.
24 Todorova (1993): 45.
25 R. E. F. Smith (1977).
26 Matossian (1982): 18.
27 Matossian (1982): 18
28 Matossian (1982): 24.
29 Czap (1982a), (1982b).
30 Hasluck *The Unwritten Law of Albania* (1954).
31 Harrington (1995).
32 Protestants also had institutions to support but on quite a different scale and without involving family strategies in the same way, more through preaching, prayer and personal discipline
33 See the novel by George Moore, *Esther Waters*
34 Hufton (1995): 105.
35 Hufton (1995): 119.
36 Hufton (1995): 145.
37 Kertzer (1984); Kertzer and Saller (1991): 9.
38 Barbagli (1991).
39 Horrell and Humphries (1995): 106.

40 Homans (1941).
41 I have not defined 'class' in this work but I use the term in a general way as a signpost to indicate broadly post-Bronze-Age systems of stratification, based on the economy. There is of course much more to be said about the concept, about the styles of life, about class milieu and mobility.
42 Jones (1985).
43 Ginsborg (1990): 76.

9 Proto and Full Industrialization

1 For Rome, see Lacey (1968); for the Carolignian period, see Coleman (1974); for later periods, see Kertzer (1993), Laslett (1977) and others
2 For the Middle Ages, see Duby (1978).
3 See Herlihy and Klapisch-Zuber (1978) for Florence; Nicholas (1985) for Ghent.
4 Tilly and Scott (1987).
5 See Bergeron (1978) and Schlumberger (1934) quoted in Goody (1996): 194–6
6 My use of English material is more shamefaced in this chapter as it relates to what is generally agreed to be the 'First Industrial Nation' Others soon followed.
7 Medick (1976): 296.
8 Medick (1976).
9 Mendels (1971).
10 Wrigley (1971).
11 Medick (1976): 313, quoting Schultess (1818).
12 Tilly and Scott (1987): 91ff.
13 Tilly and Scott (1987): 93.
14 Shorter (1975), criticized in Medick (1976).
15 Pinchbeck (1930): 2.
16 Pinchbeck (1930): 132.
17 The population rose rapidly but not uncontrollably; the rise also took different forms. In Laichingen (Germany), Medick found high fertility with high infant mortality, in the northwest Schlumbohm found low fertility and low mortality (Sabean, personal communication).
18 Horrell and Humphries (1995): 106. But that is an economist's calculation based on 'labour force participation', not on workload.
19 Macauley (1987): 5.
20 Macauley (1987): 3.
21 Macauley (1987): 5.
22 Pinchbeck (1930): 282.

23 Defoe, *Compleat English Tradesman* (1738 edn), i, 279–86, quoted Pinchbeck (1930): 283.
24 According to Pinchbeck (1930); see also Horrell and Humphries (1995); Tilly and Scott (1987).
25 Pinchbeck (1930): 313.
26 This was more common in England than France where more women were employed in the agricultural economy (Tilly and Scott 1987: 2)
27 Pinchbeck (1930): 315; Horrell and Humphries (1995).
28 Pinchbeck (1930): 149–52.
29 Lipson, *Wool and Worsted Industries*, p 6, quoted Pinchbeck (1930): 117.
30 Pinchbeck (1930): 102.
31 Pinchbeck (1920): 229.
32 Anderson (1971).
33 According to Wrigley (1971).
34 Young and Wilmott (1959) and the more recent work of Ross.
35 Tosh (1994): 189.
36 Seccombe (1993).
37 Young and Wilmott (1959), Kerr (1958) and R. T. Smith (1956).
38 Goody (1962).
39 Seccombe (1993).
40 Dowry was actually made illegal in Italy in 1870 but as elsewhere was transformed into other forms such as the provision of a house. It still exists in parts of rural Italy in the form of an elaborate trousseau.
41 Seccombe (1993).
42 Seccombe (1993): 50–51.
43 Seccombe (1993): 52–3; E. P. Thompson (1991), Menefee (1981).
44 Seccombe (1993).
45 Tosh (1994): 194.
46 Szreter (1995).
47 On discontinuity see Seccombe (1991) and Stone (1977); on continuity see Macfarlane (1978).
48 Seccombe (1993): 80.
49 Seccombe (1993): 80.
50 Szreter (1995).
51 Rublack (1995).
52 Stone (1977), Elias (1978) and Giddens (1992).
53 Cousin marriage is permitted but not frequently practised, except where property interests are still at stake
54 In Bernard Shaw's *Pygmalion*.
55 The figures are from Prost 1991: 14ff.

10   Modernization and the Family: The Theories

1   Goody (1972).
2   Stone, (1977): 268.
3   Stone (1977).
4   Stone (1977): 389.
5   Shorter (1975): 168.
6   Faucher, quoted by Pinchbeck (1930): 168.
7   Kertzer (1993).
8   Hufton (1995): 193.
9   For example Ariès (1979), Stone (1977), and Badinter (1980) who
     like Shorter (1975), perceives motherhood as the invention of capi-
     talism.
10   Hufton (1995): 206.
11   Kertzer (1993): 84.
12   Shorter (1975).
13   Stone (1977): 3.
14   See Segalen (1998).
15   Giddens (1992).
16   Stacey (1990).

11   The Contemporary Family in Practice

1   This chapter owes much to collaboration with Juliet Mitchell, the
     joint author of a forthcoming book; see our preliminary articles
     (1997) and in press (1999).
2   On this process in France, see Segalen and Zonabend (1996): 508.
3   Shorter (1975) and Badinter (1980) on the one hand, Ariès (1979)
     and Stone (1977) on the other.
4   For example Herlihy (1985) and Shorter (1975).
5   Obviously some paid work still continues at home; earlier it was with
     the sewing machine, then with the typewriter, increasingly with the
     computer, fax and phone, involving both men and women.
6   Giddens (1992).
7   For France see Segalen and Zonabend (1996): 503ff.
8   Kerblay (1996): 462–3.
9   Kerblay (1996): 463.
10   Kiernan and Wicks (1990). Single mothers are those not married to
     the father of their child; lone-parents includes all categories of parent
     living on their own.
11   Segalen and Zonabend (1996): 511.
12   Segalen and Zonabend (1996): 510.

13 See Gullestad and Segalen (eds) (1995), especially the chapter by Finch.
14 Simpson (1994).
15 Szreter (1995).
16 Sole (1975).
17 It is predicted by the UK government (January 1999) that by 2011 there will be more unmarried adults than married ones; the number of cohabiting couples will double by 2021 but that will not offset the decline in marriage (*Financial Times* 9 January 1999).
18 By Stacey (1990) and Simpson (1994) respectively.
19 Giddens (1992).
20 In the UK in 1991.

Glossary

affines	relatives by marriage.
agnatic	relationships traced through males alone (but not necessarily in the context of descent groups).
alliance	a term for marriage but usually of a repetitive kind over the generations (for example, prescriptive alliance).
bilateral	relationships traced through both parents.
Borough English	inheritance by the younger son.
Borough French	inheritance by the eldest son.
clan	a group of individuals putatively related by unilineal descent, either through males only (patrilineally in a patriclan) or through females only (matrilineal in a matriclan).
classificatory	applied to the use of kin terms that override linearity, for example, the term uncle; the opposite, in L. H. Morgan's usage, of descriptive, for example, mother's brother.
cognate	relationship of a bilateral kind (earlier in Roman law, kin who were not agnates, that is, were related by complementary filiation).
collateral	kin relationships between siblings or their descendants.
complementary filiation	relationships traced through the parent not relevant for the reckoning of unilineal descent (i.e., the mother in a patriclan).

complex families	a vague phrase used to describe households that consist of more than nuclear kin (for example, step-parents).
conjugal fund	a joint 'fund' established at marriage by the bringing together of the property of husband and wife, usually in a generalized way distinct from that of the senior generation.
consanguine	a relation through father or mother (literally, related by 'blood' as distinct from marriage).
descent	here used mainly to refer to unilineal descent (through males *or* females only) as distinct from filiation. This term is also commonly used for any perceived relationship created by procreation, including fictional procreation such as adoption.
devolution	the process of the transmission of relatively exclusive rights (especially in property) to potential heirs whether at death or between the living (i.e. including dowry and inheritance).
diverging devolution	the transfer of property, at death, at marriage or otherwise (*inter vivos*) to children of both sexes.
dower	the property to which a widow is entitled at the death of her husband.
dowry	the property transferred to a woman when she marries.
elementary or nuclear family	mother, father, children. Strictly speaking there are two for an individual, the family of orientation, into which one is born, and the family of procreation, which one establishes by marriage and by the birth of children.
emancipation	when children are no longer under the financial and jural care of the parents.
endogamy	the rule prescribing marriage within a group, especially castes in India.
epiklerate	See heiress.
exogamy	the rule prescribing marriage outside a particular group.
expanded households	those based upon sibling ties.
extended family	a vague phrase referring to interacting

relatives outside the elementary family (for example, descendants of the same grandparents).

filiacentric (or uxorilocal) union

a marriage, usually with an heiress, whereby a man joins the woman at marriage in a society where the general practice is the reverse. Sometimes called uxorilocal but that term is best reserved for a practice applying to a society as a whole.

gavelkind

the Kentish practice of equal division of the inheritance among brothers.

gens

originally a Roman patriclan, occasionally applied to any patriclan.

heiress

a woman who in the absence of brothers inherits the parental property (*epiklerate* in Greece).

household

the persons who belong to one consumption group (houseful – those who belong to one dwelling group).

hypergamy

a marriage of a woman to a man of higher class or status.

hypogamy

a marriage of a woman to a man of lower class or status.

in-marriage

marriage within a category or group, but not obligatory.

isogamy

marriage to someone of the same class or status.

joint family

usually refers to the Hindu pattern whereby a sibling group continues to hold property in common after the father's death (for example, a *frèreche*).

jural

applied to norms that are formally sanctioned but not by courts.

kin

those deemed to be related through filiation, consanguines.

kindreds

a group of kin related through males and females, either from an ancestor (or couple) in a descending kindred, or upwards from oneself (or siblings) in an ascending kindred.

late marriage

a phrase used by historial demographers to mean a marriage age of over 26 for men and over 23 for women.

levirate

the inheritance of widows by a kinsman who acts as procreator on behalf of the

	dead man (i.e., he is genitor but not pater of any children he produces).
life-cycle servants	men and women who as adolescents go into service (usually living-in) until they marry and set up their own household.
lineages	originally a medieval expression for a descent line but now used for a segmentary lineage, a group descended unilineally from an ancestor or ancestress in which the span of the lineage is related to its depth (paradigmatically the Nuer lineage).
lignages	the European version, usually found among the nobility, more a line of unilineal descent but one in which women have some rights to take out property, by the dower or as heiresses. Unilineal but not entirely as far as inheritance is concerned.
matriarchal	a vague term referring to female dominance in a variety of possible spheres, especially authority in the household.
matrifocality	applied to domestic groups that centre upon the mother, as in the Caribbean.
matrilineal	relationship of descent traced through women alone.
matrilocal	the post-marital residence is determined by the woman.
mésalliance	a marriage outside the recognized bounds, a marriage of unequals.
monogamy	the societal rule restricting marriage to a single partner.
optative	used of some northern French systems of devolution whereby individuals can either take a share of the property on leaving the household or wait to inherit at the death of a parent.
patriarchy	a vague term referring to male dominance in a variety of possible spheres, especially authority in the household.
patrilineal	a relationship of descent traced through males alone.
patronymic	a system of family (or group) names taken from the father.
peculium	the property which a wife accumulates on her own.
polygamy	where marriage is permitted to more than

one spouse simultaneously.

polygyny where a man may marry more than one wife simultaneously.

préciput (French) portion of an estate or inheritance devolving upon one of the co-heirs over and above his equal share with the others.

preferential a preferred (not obligatory) marriage, usually of a kinship kind.

primogeniture devolution to the eldest son (usually according him only preferential not exclusive treatment). Occasionally women are included (as in Basque country).

prohibited degrees the range of kin among whom marriage is forbidden.

ritual kin arrangements such as blood brotherhood or godparenthood whereby people acquire 'fictional' kin through ritual or religious means.

sibling a brother or sister by the same parents.

sororate the obligation of a widower to marry the sister of the dead wife.

spiritual kinship the Christian form of ritual or fictional kinship, godparenthood.

succession refers to the transmission of office, inheritance (or devolution) to property and descent to kinship (usually unilineal); I use it primarily for the first.

tribe a vague term used for a relatively small socio-ethnic group.

unigeniture devolution to one child alone, whether oldest or youngest, male or female.

unilineal relationship traced through men or women alone.

women's property complex the situation that exists in the major Eurasian societies whereby women participate in the devolution of family property, with all the consequences that entails for marriage and status.

Bibilography

Anderson, M. 1971. *Family Structure in Nineteenth Century Lancashire*. Cambridge.

Ariès, P. 1962 [1979]. *Centuries of Childhood*. New York.

Badinter, E. 1980 *L'Amour en plus: histoire de l'amour maternel – XVIIᵉ–XXᵉ siècle*. Paris.

Banfield, E. C. 1958. *The Moral Basis of a Backward Society*. Glencoe, Ill.

Barbagli, M. 1991. Three household formation systems in eighteenth- and nineteenth-century Italy. In D. I. Kertzer and R. P. Saller (eds), *The Family in Italy from Antiquity to the Present*. New Haven.

Benveniste, E. 1969. *Le Vocabulaire des institutions indo-européennes*, vol. 1. Paris.

Bernand, C. and Gruzinski, S. 1996. Children of the Apocalypse: the family in Meso-America and the Andes. In A. Burgière et al. (eds), *A History of the Family*, vol. II. Cambridge.

Boswell, J. 1988. *Kindness to Strangers: the abandonment of children in Western Europe from Late Antiquity to the Renaissance*. New York.

Bremmer, J. and van den Bosch, L. (eds) 1994. *Between Poverty and the Pyre: moments in the history of widowhood*. London.

Brettel, C. B. 1991. Property, kinship and gender: a Mediterranean perspective. In D. I. Kertzer and R. P. Saller (eds), *The Family in Italy from Antiquity to the Present*. New Haven.

Chaytor, M. 1980. Household and kinship: Ryton in the late 16th and early 17th centuries. *History Workshop Journal* 10: 25–60.

Coleman, E. 1974. L'infanticide dans le haut moyen Age. *Annales ESC* 29: 315–35.

Corbier, M. 1991. Constructing kinship in Rome: marriage and divorce, filiation and adoption. In D. I. Kertzer and R. P. Saller (eds), *The Family in Italy from Antiquity to the Present*. New Haven.

Couroucli, M. 1985. *Les Oliviers du ligneage*. Paris.

Czap, P. 1982a. A large family: the peasant's greatest wealth. In R. Wall, J. Robin and P. Laslett (eds), *Family Forms in Historic Europe*. Cambridge.

—— 1982b. The perennial multiple family household: Mishino, Russia, 1782–1858. *Journal of Family History* 7: 8–26.

Davis, J. 1973. *Land and Family in Pisticci*. London.

Davis, N. Z. 1995. *Women on the Margins: three seventeenth-century lives*. Boston.

Duby, G. 1978. *Medieval Marriage: two models from twelfth-century France*. Baltimore.

Dumont, L. 1981. La genèse chrétienne de l'individualisme: une vue modifiée de nos origines. *Le Débat* 15: 124–46.

Elias, N. 1978. *The Civilising Process*. Oxford.

Engels, F. [1972]. *The Origin of the Family, Private Property and the State*. London.

Ferrante, L. 1996. Marriage and women's subjectivity in a patrilineal system: the case of early modern Bologna. In M. J. Maynes et al. (eds), *Gender, Kinship, Power: a comparative and interdisciplinary history*. New York.

Flandrin, J. F. 1979 [1976]. *Families in Former Times: kinship, household and sexuality*. Cambridge.

Galt, A. H. 1991a. Marital property in an Apulian town during the eighteenth and early nineteenth centuries. In D. I. Kertzer and R. P. Saller (eds), *The Family in Italy from Antiquity to the Present*. New Haven.

—— 1991b. *Far from the Church Bells: settlement and society in an Apulian town*. Cambridge.

Garnsey, P. 1991. Child rearing in ancient Italy. In D. I. Kertzer and R. P. Saller (eds), *The Family in Italy from Antiquity to the Present*. New Haven.

Gaunt, D. 1983. The property and kin relationships of retired farmers in Northern and Central Europe. In R. Wall et al. (eds), *Family Forms in Historic Europe*. Cambridge.

Giddens, A. 1992. *The Transformation of Intimacy: love and eroticism in modern societies*. Oxford.

Gies, F. and J. 1987. *Marriage and the Family in the Middle Ages*. New York.

Ginsborg, P. 1990. *A History of Contemporary Italy: society and politics 1943–1988*. Harmondsworth, Middlesex.

Goody, J. 1962. *Death, Property and the Ancestors*. Stanford.

—— (ed.) 1966. *Succession to High Office*. Cambridge.

—— 1972. The evolution of the family. In P. Laslett and R. Wall (eds), *Household and Family in Past Time*. Cambridge.

—— 1976. *Production and Reproduction: a comparative study of the domestic domain*. Cambridge.

—— 1983. *The Development of the Family and Marriage in Europe*. Cambridge.

—— 1990. *The Oriental, the Ancient and the Primitive*. Cambridge.

—— 1996. *The East in the West*. Cambridge.

Greilsammer, M. 1990. *L'Envers du tableau: mariage et maternité en Flandre médiévale*. Paris.

Guichard, P. 1977. *Structures sociales 'orientales' et 'occidentales' dans l'Espagne musulmane*. Paris.

—— and Cuvillier, J.-P. 1996. Barbarian Europe. In A. Burgière et al. (eds), *A History of the Family*, vol. 1. (Fr. edn. 1986). Cambridge.

Gullestad, M. and Segalen, M. (eds) 1995. *La Famille en Europe: parenté et perpétuation familiale*. Paris.

Hajnal, J. 1982. Two kinds of pre-industrial household formation systems. *Population and Development Review* 8: 449–94.

Hammel, E. A. 1972. The *zadruga* as process. In P. Laslett and R. Wall (eds), *Household and Family in Past Time*. Cambridge.

Hanawalt, B. 1986. *The Ties that Bound: peasant families in medieval London*. New York.

—— 1993. *Growing up in Medieval London: the experience of childhood in history*. New York.

—— 1996. Patriachal provisions for widows and orphans in medieval London. In M. J. Maynes et al. (eds), *Gender, Kinship, Power: a comparative and interdisciplinary history*. New York.

Harrington, J. E. 1995. *Reordering Marriage and Society in Reformation Germany*. Cambridge.

Hasluck, M. 1954. *The Unwritten Law of Albania*. Cambridge.

Herlihy, D. 1985. *Medieval Households*. Cambridge, MA.

—— and Klapisch-Zuber, C. 1978. *Les Toscans et leurs familles: une étude du 'catasto' florentin de 1427*. Paris.

Hill, B. 1989. The marriage age of women and the demographers. *History Workshop Journal* 28: 129–47.

Hodges, R. 1982. *Dark Age Economics: the origin of towns and trade* AD *600–1000*. London.

Homans, G. C. 1941. *English Villagers of the Thirteenth Century*. Cambridge, MA.

Horrel, S. and Humphries, J. 1995. Women's labour force participation and the transition to the male-breadwinner family, 1790–1865. *Economic History Review* 48: 89–117.

Hufton, O. 1995. *The Prospect before Her: a history of women in Western Europe*, vol. 1, *1500–1800*. London.

—— 1998. The widow's mite and other strategies: funding the Catholic reformation. *Transactions of the Royal Historical Society*, forthcoming.

Ingram, M. 1987. *Church Courts, Sex and Marriage in England, 1570–1640*. Cambridge.

Jones, P. M. 1985. *Politics in the Rural Society in the southern Massif Central c. 1750–1880*. Cambridge.

Kerblay, B. 1996. Socialist families. In A. Burgière et al. (eds), *A History of the Family*, vol. II. Cambridge.

Kerr, M. 1958. *The People of Ship Street*. London.

Kertzer, D. I. and Saller, R. P. (eds) 1984. *Family Life in Central Italy*. New Brunswick.

—— and —— 1991. *The Family in Italy from Antiquity to the Present*. New Haven.

—— and —— 1993. *Sacrificed for Honor: Italian infant abandonment and the politics of reproductive control*. Boston.

Kiernan, K. and Wicks, M. 1990. *Family Change and Future Policy*. London: Family Policy Studies Centre.

King, P. D. 1972. *Law and Society in the Visigothic Kingdom*. Cambridge.

Kirshner, J. 1991. Materials for a gilded cage: non-dotal assets in Florence, 1300–1500. In D. I. Kertzer and R. P. Saller (eds), *The Family in Italy from Antiquity to the Present*. New Haven.

Klapisch-Zuber, C. 1985. *Women, Family and Ritual in Renaissance Italy*. Chicago.

—— 1991. Kinship and politics in fourteenth-century Florence. In D. I. Kertzer and R. P. Saller (eds), *The Family in Italy from Antiquity to the Present*. New Haven.

—— 1996. Family trees and the construction of kinship in Renaissance Italy. In M. J. Maynes et al. (eds), *Gender, Kinship, Power: a comparative and interdisciplinary history*. New York.

Lacey, W. K. 1968. *The Family in Classical Greece*. London.

Laslett, P. 1972. Mean household size in England since the sixteenth century. In P. Laslett and R. Wall (eds), *Household and Family in Past Time*. Cambridge.

—— 1976. Familie und Industrialisierung, eine starke theorie. In W. Conze (ed.), *Sozial Geschichte der Familie in der Neuzeit Europes*. Stuttgart.

—— 1977. *Family Life and Illicit Love in Earlier Generations*. Cambridge.

—— and Wall, R. (eds) 1972. *Household and Family in Past Times*. Cambridge.

Le Goff, J. 1990. Preface to M. Greilsammer, *L'Envers du tableau: mariage et maternité en Flandre médiévale*. Paris.

Loizos, P. 1975. *The Greek Gift: politics in a Cypriot Village*. Oxford.

Lynch, J. H. 1986. *Godparents and Kinship in Early Medieval Europe.* Princeton, NJ.

McCabe, R. A. 1993. *Incest, Drama and Nature's Law 1550–1700.* Cambridge.

Macaulay, R. 1987. *'Dull dejection in the countenances of all of them': children at work in the Rhode Island textile industry.* Slater Mill Historic Site, Pawtucket.

MacCormack 1997. Sin, citizenship and the salvation of souls: the impact of Christian priorities on late-Roman and post-Roman society. *Comparative Studies in Society and History,* 39: 646–73.

Macfarlane, A. 1970. *The Diary of Ralph Josselin, 1616–1685.* Oxford.

—— 1978. *The Origins of English Individualism: family, property and social transition.* Oxford.

—— 1986. *Marriage and Love in England 1300–1840.* Cambridge.

Maine, H. S. 1861. *Ancient Law* (1955 edn). London.

Malinowski, B. 1913. *The Family among the Australian Aborigines: a sociological study.* London.

Martin, C. 1995. *Qui Doit Nourir l'enfant quand les parents sont séparés? Le Père, la mère et l'Etat providence: une comparaison France–Angleterre.* In N. Lefaucher and C. Martin, *Qui doit nourir l'enfant dont le père est 'absent'?* TRASS, Paris.

Matossian, M. 1982. The peasant way of life. In W. S. Vicinich (ed.), *The Peasant in Nineteenth-Century Russia.* Stanford.

Maynes, M. J. 1996. Women and kinship in propertyless classes in Western Europe in the nineteenth century. In M. J. Maynes et al. (eds), *Gender, Kinship, Power: a comparative and interdisciplinary history.* New York.

Medick, H. 1976. The proto-industrial family economy; the structural function of household and family during the transition from peasant society to industrial capitalism. *Social History* 3: 291–316.

—— (with P. Kriedke and J. Schlumbohm) 1981. *Industrialization before Industrialization: rural industry in the genesis of capitalism.* Cambridge.

Mendels, F. 1971. Industrialization and population pressure in eighteenth-century Flanders. *Journal of Economic History* 31: 269–71.

Menefee, S. B. 1981. *Wives for Sale: an ethnographic study of British popular divorce.* Oxford.

Mitchell, J. and Goody, J. 1997. Feminism, fatherhood and the family in late twentieth-century Britain. In A. Oakley and J. Mitchell (eds), *Who's Afraid of Feminism?* London.

—— In press. Family or familiarity? In M. Richards et al. (eds), *What is a Parent?* Oxford.

Mitterauer, M. and Sieder, R. 1982. *The European Family: patriarchy to partnership from the middle ages to the present.* Oxford.

Mundy, J. H. 1991. *Europe in the High Middle Ages, 1156–1309* (2nd edn). London.

Murray, A. 1983. *Germanic Kinship Structure: studies in law and society in antiquity and the early Middle Ages.* Toronto.

Nicholas, D. 1985. *The Domestic Life of a Medieval City: women, children, and the family in fourteenth-century Ghent.* Nebraska.

Okely, J. 1983. *The Traveller-gypsies.* Cambridge.

Ozouf, M. 1995. *Les Mots des femmes: essai sur la singularité française.* Paris.

Peristiany, J. G. and Pitt-Rivers, J. (eds) 1991. *Honour and Grace in Anthropology.* Cambridge.

Phillpots, B. 1913. *Kindred and Clan in the Middle Ages and After: a study in the sociology of the Teutonic races.* Cambridge.

—— 1931. *Edda and Sagon.* London.

Pinchbeck, I. 1930. *Women Workers and the Industrial Revolution 1750–1850* (2nd edn, 1969). London.

Pomata, G. 1996. Blood ties and semen ties: consanguinity and cognition in Roman law. In M. J. Maynes et al. (eds), *Gender, Kinship, Power: a comparative and interdisciplinary history.* New York.

Prost, A. 1991. Public and private spheres in France. In A. Prost and G. Vincent (eds), *Riddles of Identity in Modern Times*, vol V, *A History of Private Life* (general eds P. Aries and G. Duby). Cambridge, MA.

Ravis-Giordani, G. 1994. Introduction générale. *L'Ile-Familles, Etudes Corses* 22: 7–17.

Rawson, B. (ed.) 1986. *The Family in Ancient Rome: new perspectives.* New York.

—— 1991. *Marriage, Divorce and Children in Ancient Rome.* Canberra.

Razi, Z. 1980. *Life, Marriage and Death in a Medieval Parish: economy, society and demography in Halesowen 1270–1400.* Cambridge.

—— 1982. Family, land and the village community in later Medieval England. *Past and Present* 93: 3–36.

Roper, L. 1994. *Oedipus and the Devil: witchcraft, sexuality and religion in early modern Europe.* London.

Rowland, R. 1986. Sistemas matrimonialas en la peninsula ibérica (siglos XVI–XIX): una perspectiva regional. In P. V. Moreda and D. S. Reher (eds), *La Demografíca Histórica de la Peninsula Ibérica.* Madrid.

Rublack, U. 1995. Viehisch, Freeh und onverschämpt: inzest in Südwest deutschland, ca. 1530–1700. In O. Ulbricht (ed), *Von Huren und Robenmüttern: weibliche kriminalität in der Frühen Neuzeit.* Cologne.

Sabean, D. W. 1990. *Property, Production, and Family in Neckarhausen 1700–1870.* Cambridge.

Saller, R. 1991. European family history and Roman law. *Continuity and Change* 36: 335–46.

Seccombe, W. 1990. Starting to stop: working-class fertility decline in Britain. *Past and Present* 126: 151–88.

—— 1991. *A Millennium of Social Changes: from feudalism to capitalism in north western Europe*. London.

—— 1993. *Weathering the Storm: working class families from the Industrial Revolution to the fertility decline*. London.

Segalen, M. 1981. *Sociologie de la famille*. Paris.

—— 1996. The Industrial Revolution: from proletariat to bourgeoisie. In A. Burgière et al. (eds), *A History of the Family*, vol. II. Cambridge.

—— and Zonabend, F. 1996. Families in France. In A. Burgière et al. (eds), *A History of the Family*, vol. II. Cambridge.

Shahar, S. 1990. *Childhood in the Middle Ages*. London.

Shaw, B. 1991. The cultural meaning of death: age and gender in the Roman family. In D. I. Kertzer and R. P. Saller (eds), *The Family in Italy from Antiquity to the Present*. New Haven.

—— and Saller, R. P. 1984. Close-kin marriages in Roman society. *Man* 19: 432–44.

Sheehan, M. N. 1963. The influence of Canon Law on the property rights of married women in England. *Mediaeval Studies 25*.

—— 1991. Sexuality, marriage, celibacy and the family in Central and Northern Italy: Christian legal and moral guides in the Early Middle Ages. In D. I. Kertzer and R. P. Saller (eds), *The Family and Italy from Antiquity to the Present*. New Haven.

Shorter, E. 1975. *The Making of the Modern Family*. New York.

Simpson, R. 1994. Bringing the *unclear* family into focus: divorce and re-marriage in contemporary Britain. *Man* 29: 831–51.

Smith, R. E. F. 1977. *Peasant Farming in Muscovy*. Cambridge.

Smith, R. M. 1979. Some reflections on the evidence for the origin of the 'European marriage pattern' in England. In C. Harris (ed), *The Sociology of the Family*. Keele.

Smith, R. T. 1956. *The Negro Family in British Guiana: family structure and social status in the villages*. London.

Solé, J. 1976. *L'Amour en Occident à l'époque moderne*. Paris.

Stacey, J. 1990. *Brave New Families: stories of domestic upheaval in late-twentieth-century America*. New York.

Stewart, M. 1997. *The Time of the Gypsies*. Oxford.

Stone, L. 1977. *Family, Sex and Marriage in England 1500–1800*. London.

—— 1986. 'Illusions of a changeless family', review of Alan Macfarlane, *Marriage and Love in England*. *Times Literary Supplement*, 16 May 1986: 525.

—— 1988. Passionate attachments in the west in historical perspective. In W. Gaylin and E. S. Person (eds), *Passionate Attachments*. New York.

—— 1992. *Road to Divorce, England 1530–1987*. Oxford.

Szreter, S. 1995. *Fertility, Class and Gender in Britain, 1860–1940*. Cambridge.

Tadmor, N. 1996. The concept of the household – family in eighteenth-century England. *Past and Present* 151: 111–73.

Thompson, E. P. 1991. The sale of wives. In *Customs in Common*. London.

Thompson, G. D. 1949. *Studies in Ancient Greek Society: the prehistoric Aegean*. London.

Tilley, L. A. and Scott, J. W. 1987. *Women, Work and Family*. London.

Todd, M. 1972. *Everyday Life of the Barbarians: Goths, Franks and Vandals*. London.

Todorova, M. N. 1993. *Balkan Family Structure and the European Pattern: demographic developments in Ottoman Bulgaria*. Washington, D.C.

Tosh, J. 1994. What should historians do with masculinity? *History Workshop Journal* 38: 179–202.

Treggiari, S. 1991. *Roman Marriage: iusti coniuges from the time of Cicero to the time of Ulpian*. Oxford.

Veyne, P. 1978. La famille et l'amour dans le haut empire romain. *Annales E.S.C.* 33: 35–63.

Wall, R. (ed.) 1988. *The Upheaval of War: family, work and welfare in Europe, 1914–1918*. Cambridge.

Wemple, S. 1981. *Women in Frankish Society: marriage and the cloister, 500–900*. Philadelphia.

Wickham, C. 1994. *Land and Power: studies in Italian and European social history, 400–1200*. London.

Wolf, E. R. 1966. *Peasants*. Englewood Cliffs, NJ.

Wrightson, K. 1981. Household and kinship in sixteenth-century England. *History Workshop Journal*: 151–8.

—— 1998. The family in early modern England: continuity and change. In S. Taylor et al. (eds), *Hanoverian Britain and Empire: essays in memory of Philip Lawson*. Ipswich.

Wrigley, E. A. 1971. The process of modernization and the industrial revolution in England. *Journal of Interdisciplinary History* 3: 225–60.

Young, M. and Wilmott, P. 1959. *Family and Kinship in East London*. London.

Yver, J. 1966. *Egalité entre héritiers et exclusion des enfants dotés: essai de géographie coutumière*. Paris.

Zborowski, M. and Herzog, E. 1952. *Life is with People: the culture of the shtetl*. New York.

Selected Reading

Anderson, M. 1990. *Approaches to the History of the Family, 1500–1914*. London.

Attias-Donfut, C. and Segalen, M. 1998. *Grands-parents: la famille à travers les générations*. Paris.

Bordet, J.-P. and Dupaquier, J. 1997. *Histoire des populations de l'Europe*, vol. 1. *Des Origines aux prémices de la révolution demographique*. Paris.

Burgière, A. et al. (eds) 1996 [1986]. *A History of the Family*. Cambridge.

Flandrin, J.-F. 1979. *Families in Former Times: kinship household, and sexuality*. Cambridge.

Goody, J. 1983. *The Development of the Family and Marriage in Europe*. Cambridge.

Herlihy, D. 1985. *Medieval Households*. Cambridge, MA.

Hufton, O. 1995. *The Prospect before Her: a history of women in Western Europe*, vol. 1, *1500–1800*. London.

Laslett, P. 1965. *The World We Have Lost*. London.

Macfarlane, A. 1986. *Marriage and Love in England, 1300–1840*. Cambridge.

Mitterauer, M. and Seider, R. 1982. *The European Family: patriachy to partnership from the middle ages to the present*. Oxford.

Phillips, R. 1988. *Putting Asunder: a history of divorce in western society*. Cambridge.

Seccombe, W. 1991. *A Millennium of Social Changes: from feudalism to capitalism in north western Europe*. London.

—— 1993. *Weathering the Storm: working class families from the Industrial Revolution to the fertility decline*. London.

Segalen, M. 1981. *Sociologie de la Famille*. Paris.
Stone, L. 1977. *Family, Sex and Marriage in England 1500–1800*.
    London.

Index

Page numbers in bold type indicate main or detailed references